The German Comedy

The German Comedy

• • • • •

SCENES OF LIFE AFTER THE WALL

Peter Schneider

TRANSLATED BY PHILIP BOEHM
AND LEIGH HAFREY

Farrar Straus Giroux

NEW YORK

Printed in the United States of America
First published in 1991 by Farrar, Straus and Giroux

Designed by Victoria Wong
Fifth printing, 1999
Excerpts from this book have appeared in *The New York Times
Magazine* and *Harper's Magazine*.

We wish to thank Elliot Rabin for the right to consult
"Concrete and Irony."

Library of Congress Cataloging-in-Publication Data
Schneider, Peter.
[Extreme Mittellage. English]
The German comedy : scenes of life after the wall / Peter
Schneider ; translated by Philip Boehm and Leigh Hafrey.
p. cm.
Translation of : Extreme Mittellage.
1. Germany—Description and travel—1945–   I. Title.
DD43.S31613 1991 943.087—dc20 91-20416 CIP

Contents

♦ ♦ ♦ ♦ ♦

Preface

Once the improbable had happened, it seemed so obvious. After all, did the East German regime really have any choice but to open the Berlin Wall, given the flood of refugees that had been swelling from week to week and surging to the West? In fact, didn't they tear the Wall down for the same reason they put it up twenty-nine years earlier—to keep people *in*? The strategy was bound to fail—and it did, twice. So why was anyone surprised?

Over the decades, a lot of smart people said a lot of smart things about the problem of partition and the possibility of resolving it. But the simple truth is that almost all of them were wrong when it came to the how and the when of a solution. In the case of Germany, events contradicted practically every historical prediction.

German political parties are now vying daily for the glory of having brought down the Wall. Many famous and not-so-famous jockeys claim to have ridden the horse that, to everyone's astonishment, jumped the infamous obstacle and reached the finish line called unity. At the end of the race, however, none of the claimants was in the saddle. No one had ridden the winning horse; no one had guided it. After a few yards, it simply left the established course and, with neither bit nor saddle nor rider, sped toward a goal of its own making.

But who was behind it all? Mikhail Gorbachev? No one will disagree that, with *perestroika* and *glasnost*, and, most of all, with his explicit rejection of force, Gorbachev set off the avalanche of revolutionary change. But did he know what he was unleashing? I'm sure Gorbachev intended to free the European satellite countries—even East Germany—of Soviet hegemony, but did he mean for East Germany to simply disappear from the political map of the world and be absorbed into its West German brother state? Once he had rejected the option of military intervention, the only thing he could really anticipate with any certainty was that he couldn't anticipate or direct anything anymore. The tanks Gorbachev sent into the Baltic republics in January of 1991 were only a late proof that history had far outrun his intentions.

What about Helmut Kohl? In my opinion, the West German chancellor has been unfairly accused of whipping the Germans into unity. In truth, he merely followed—with amazing agility and presence of mind—the majority of East Germans who were tired of socialism and wanted unity now and at any cost.

So then what about the East German people? Certainly, they were history's agent if anyone was. But did they know where their protest was going, and when and how it would stop? Or were they merely applying the lesson everyone learns under socialism: Buy it now if you can—tomorrow the shop window will be empty.

So far, so bad, but the question remains: If it wasn't Mikhail Gorbachev, and if it wasn't Helmut Kohl, or even the East German people—who was it? Who brought about the political miracle—or disaster—of German unity? This seems to be where faith begins, at least according to an announcement that appeared in the *Weinstadt Woche*, a local Christian Democrat newspaper: "On October 3, a dream became reality. Germany is reunited. Just a year ago, no German politician was pursuing this goal, and no foreign politician wanted it. So no human being can take credit for having brought Germany together—it was God's work. God has forgiven us our guilt for the murder of six million Jews."

The problem with the "God" hypothesis, of course, is that "God" rarely speaks for himself, and much too frequently in the voices of questionable interpreters. Having never been mistaken for a prophet myself, I doubt it was God who gave the Germans unity. It seems that history has moved on its own here, without any plan, divine or mortal, drawing on the most varied political forces with little discrimination, taking from the left and the right, from villains and heroes, from East and West.

The untamed appearance of events reminds all of us—winners, losers, and observers alike—that we never fully plan or control history. If it is subject to any laws, they certainly aren't "iron"; it would be more appropriate to say that they are as light as a feather and extremely fragile.

Preface

The delicate working of these elusive forces in everyday life has been my subject for many years. In *The Wall
Jumper* I took the measure of the mental wall that kept
Germans divided. *The German Comedy* is about a coming together, generally a happier process than parting,
but no less fraught with misunderstanding. How this
remarriage will work after forty years of separation,
whether the two partners will ever make a happy couple,
and how the neighbors will feel about it—we shall have
to see.

My thanks to Sara Bershtel and André Schiffrin who
urged me to write this book.

The German
Comedy

* * * * *

Before the Fall

Was Ronald Reagan really the only one with eyes in his head? Was he the only one who could read the writing on Berlin's hundred-mile Wall when he cried out in the spring of 1987: "Mr. Gorbachev, tear down this wall!"?

Berliners are used to political fanfare, and they applauded Reagan's appeal more out of duty than enthusiasm. The demand to tear down the Wall was as old as the Wall itself; it had, in one form or another, become part of diplomatic protocol for every state visit. No one who demanded it really needed to worry that he might be taken seriously. But Reagan was different, not only because he shot from the hip, but also because he was aiming at a new target. When Mikhail Gorbachev became the Kremlin's number one man, simultaneous interpreters in both the East and the West suddenly started running into a problem: they could no longer predict the new general secretary's replies and were forced to wait until he finished each sentence. Did the president of the United States realize his demand would be met within a mere two and a half years, and did he anticipate the consequences?

Only the Great Communicator himself can answer that question, and it's likely he doesn't remember exactly what he was thinking but not saying at the time.

Years ago, I heard a member of West Germany's permanent mission to East Berlin make a heretical comment that has stayed with me ever since: "Sometimes I think the Wall is the only thing that still keeps us Germans together."

Although I didn't take this to mean he accepted the principle of two German states, I did hear the implicit questions in his remark: Can Germans still claim a common identity after forty years of partition or are there now two different German ways of living and thinking? Is the Wall the only argument left for the theory of a common German identity? In short, hadn't the concrete Wall long ago become a symbol, a symbol of the wall inside our heads?

At least since early 1989 there had been signs, fine cracks in the cement suggesting that the Wall might soon open. And through the cracks one could see the shadows of things to come, the new conflicts and constellations that would unfold once the Wall came tumbling down.

Just a few hundred yards from the Brandenburg Gate, where Reagan had made his urgent plea to Gorbachev, a flea market appeared in the spring of 1989. Since January of that year, the Polish regime had been making it easier for its citizens to travel to West Berlin. And so the Poles came, as many as 8,000 a weekend—by train, by bus, by Polski-Fiat—to peddle their wares out of plastic bags and suitcases. They held what they had to sell in their two hands: a bottle of vodka in the left, a pair of baby's stockings in the right. They were selling all the things the West had too much of and the East too little: children's clothes, butter, sausages, chocolate, dill pickles, handsaws, soldering irons, underwear, cigarettes. They came in response to the black market rate for German marks back home: a Polish trader who made forty marks' profit in a weekend could exchange that sum for a month's wages in zlotys.

In a matter of days, the deserted borderland along the Wall near Potsdamer Platz, once the busiest square in Europe, was repopulated; to many West Berliners, the area had acquired a slightly "Asian" look. It was as though, overnight, Berlin had slid 300 miles to the east. Or, from another perspective, as though Berlin had finally returned to where it lay before its westward drift after 1949. The flea market reminded Berliners of something they had forgotten, namely, that their city is twice as far from West Germany as it is from Poland: it takes barely an hour by car to reach the Polish border from Berlin. So the Polish market in West Berlin presaged a certain normalization. Of course, everything required regulation: there were vendors' taxes to collect, customs guidelines and health measures to observe, but such problems are—and were—easy to solve, at least in principle. If anyone had grounds for complaint, it was Poles with a sense of history. Wasn't it awful, they asked, that we were on the winning side forty-five years ago and now we're running to Berlin to peddle goods we don't have in Poland? So in the end, who really lost the war?

But Berliners complained the loudest. They felt threatened by the Wall's new porosity. The almost forgotten phrase "Polish housekeeping"—meaning chaos and disorder—resurfaced. A few people said outright what they didn't like about the Wall: it wasn't solid enough. Finally people saw, and admitted to seeing, how good they had it living in the western shadow of the Wall. It cost nothing to assail the oddity as a "Wall of Shame," so long as its builders in the East maintained it and made sure it had no holes. Suddenly West Berliners had to deal with this new problem on their own—but how?

Citizens suffering from Polish stress showed their displeasure by honking when a driver with Polish plates moved too slowly. If you're going to stray into Germany, you'd better know your way around. At first, officials had no idea how to handle this peaceful invasion from a neighboring country. After having expressed outrage over every bullet ever fired along the Wall, they could hardly protest now if people occasionally made it over the same obstruction. But they soon solved their problem. Poring over the law books, they came upon the term "black market," which gave West Berlin police the grounds they needed to inspect Polish car trunks and turn back traders at the border if they had any goods that required a permit. Still, it wasn't like the good old days of the Wall.

Whenever Germans have what they consider a problem, the first thing they do is build a fence. And so, two months after the Poles arrived, a rugged, prefabricated wire cage enclosed the space at Potsdamer Platz. On the fence, brand-new signs in Polish and German bore the internationally recognized word VERBOTEN. The construction crew had driven rectangular bollards of dressed stone into the sidewalk in front of the fence, to keep people from walking there, or lingering. The unmarked, upright stones suddenly made the pavement look just like a military cemetery.

When I passed by in April 1989, I wondered what secret they could be hiding in that empty space beyond the fence. What were they guarding in there?

Through the wire grid I could see the Wall. The Western fence was more delicate, more elegant than the concrete Eastern Wall, but it was clear that the one had inspired the other. It looked undeniably like plagiarism. And the fence stood so close to the mother Wall that an East German border guard in his tower was bound to feel he was being fenced in from the West. As some of the men in gray uniforms focused their binoculars on the construction work to the west, they must silently have been priming themselves for a new boss. And the fact is, the West Berlin fence reminded many people of a bad joke then making the rounds in West Berlin bars: "If they tear down the Wall in the East, we'll just put it up again a little to the west."

In a relatively harmless way, the uproar over the Polish market exposed one of the white lies of West German politics since the Second World War. I say harmless because the Polish weekend vendors went home on Sunday evening. But for the hundreds of thousands of German and "ethnic German" resettlers from the East who had been knocking on the Wall for decades and were

now suddenly being let through, that wasn't the case.
They came on a one-way ticket and said—rightly—
"Well, you invited us."

Although West Germany was the most densely pop-
ulated country in Europe after Holland and Belgium,
the half-state had, since its founding, guaranteed to any
German who wanted or was able to come over the Wall
a passport and all the rights that accrued to a citizen of
the Federal Republic. (The fact is that, despite the dis-
comforts of resettlement, the new arrivals from the East
received benefits that poorer natives had good reason to
envy: "welcome money," "adjustment aid," preferential
treatment in obtaining housing, and pension credits—
one credit for every year they worked in a Communist
country, with the result that the average resettler could
in some cases claim a higher benefit than the West German native who paid into the system.) In theory, this
blithe offer of citizenship applied not just to seventeen
million East Germans, but to some four and a half million
ethnic Germans in Poland, Hungary, the Soviet Union,
and Romania as well. According to the authorities, ethnic
Germans are Germans who have no passport, but have
maintained their German identity in foreign—read Communist—countries. It sounds innocent enough, but how
does a Romanian or Russian German prove his German
identity?

A friend from Romania—she speaks fluent German
and had been arrested numerous times as a dissident in
her home country—couldn't convince the German authorities of her German identity. Livid with rage, she
asked whether she ought to mention that her father had

been in the SS and that her uncle had died serving the same organization. They responded coolly that proof of that sort would help. Anywhere else in the world, you'd do better to hide your father's Nazi Party papers—but in Germany they still had their uses.

Long before the Wall opened, the Federal Republic's immigration policy revealed an embarrassing legacy of the supposedly buried past. Instead of establishing a realistic quota that would apply to everyone—including non-German refugees from lands Germany once laid waste—the policy gave preferential treatment to foreigners with a claim to "Germanhood."

From the beginning, it should have been obvious that the Federal Republic's invitation to all Germans would remain heartfelt only so long as the East German authorities kept the masses of potential guests away. When the Wall became more porous with Gorbachev's *glasnost*, the West Germans' joy at reuniting declined visibly. They paled when they saw how many people they'd invited. Two hundred thousand ethnic German resettlers arrived in 1988, and about 350,000 in 1989, and that doesn't include the East German refugees. In 1990, between 400,000 and 450,000 ethnic Germans "came home," as the West Germans put it, and immigration authorities now fear that, as their native economies collapse, millions more ethnic Germans from the Soviet Union and Eastern Europe may remember their German origins.

West German authorities gritted their teeth and hailed the influx as a success. Right-wing politicians deflected the growing popular anger onto the smallest group of immigrants: the non-Germans, the asylum-seekers. But the electorate wouldn't make the distinction between good German resettlers and bad foreign asylum-seekers. As early as spring 1989, a Mannheim research group began referring to the growing "confusion": the term "foreigner" had come to include German resettlers from the East and really meant "anything from outside."

At that point, they hadn't done any research on the degree to which the fear of foreign influence extended to our "brothers and sisters" from East Germany. But there were many indications that a good number of West German citizens had long since silently recognized East Germany as a separate country, fulfilling that regime's heartfelt desire. No one wanted to admit it, but we saw and treated East Germans as foreigners; in fact, according to polls, a majority of young people defined East Germany as a foreign country. This attitude became more and more evident as Chief Wall Protector Erich Honecker let increasing numbers of East Germans emigrate to the "drug culture in the West": 23,000 in 1987, 40,000 in 1988, 360,000 the year the Wall was opened. With two million people out of work in West Germany, the newcomers weren't exactly welcomed with open arms. Many of their Western compatriots spoke out angrily against the crush from the East and started using a slogan that soon appeared on Berlin sweatshirts: "Give me back my good old Wall!"

At that time, I found myself wondering whether the wire fence built near the Wall to keep out the Poles wasn't meant for East Germans as well. After all, did anyone really expect all trace of difference to vanish after forty years of division into such radically different societies—especially when people on both sides were so devoted to the same cult of obedience?

In fact, many differences were evident long before November 9, and one of the greatest concerned the question of unity. Here, popular attitudes ran exactly counter to the official line. For example, the West German regime considered itself the guardian of the German Question, and in this role, the Federal Republic celebrated two unusual national holidays, July 17 and August 13. The first commemorated the popular uprising of 1953 in which our Eastern compatriots had risked their necks, while the second mourned the construction of the Wall, an event that caused suffering primarily to the other Germans. In both cases, we were expressing the feelings of our relatives on the other side of the Wall, not our own. Since both holidays occurred during the summer, their main effect was to increase revenues for the beer and sausage industries. So I never understood why many of my friends from other Western countries should be concerned that, once the opportunity presented itself, West Germans might swap their ties to the West for the mess of pottage called reunification. In fact, I found West Germans' lack of real interest in the German Question rather alarming. It took visitors from abroad to remind us how unnatural the Wall was, how unbearable. When tourists voiced their horror at the Wall, their cries echoed our own from years before, when the wound was still fresh.

Almost none of these attitudes and emotions were

shared by Germans living behind the Wall; or, to be more precise, they were completely inverted. Shortly after Erich Honecker assumed power in 1974, all references to reunification as something possible or desirable were stricken from the East German constitution. To be sure, at that time the partition of Germany was a quarter century old and seemed irrevocable. August 13, the West German day of mourning, became a day of national jubilation in the East which all those imprisoned by the Wall were urged to celebrate. As a result, that day became a ghostly, pan-German spectacle Berliners could follow on both East and West German television. The West German network carried footage of the Christian Democrats' Youth Group, defiantly swinging banners and demonstrating—completely dry-eyed—beside the graves of people who had been shot jumping the Wall. One width of the Wall away from the same spot, East German TV showed factory brigades laying wreaths on the graves of border police who had "died in the line of duty." As in the West, the official line on the German Question ran directly counter to people's actual feelings on the subject. Naturally, there were no published surveys on how many eighteen-to-twenty-five-year-old East Germans considered West Germany a "foreign" country and felt the German Question had been "resolved," which is what Erich Honecker would have liked. But the assertion that most people thought so would certainly have struck everyone as laughably blatant propaganda.

So there were ample signs that Germans felt the exact opposite of what their regimes maintained. In the West, the official mourning over the Wall played to an empty house. In the East, the incessant claims that the German Question had been resolved only proved that it had not. In short, most, if not all, West Germans saw things the way Honecker was vainly commanding his subjects to, while the East Germans harbored the strong desire for reunification that Helmut Kohl was urging without success on his Germans. Thus the prognosis for the day the Wall came tumbling down was that Germans would discover they differed more than they agreed. After forty years of living under such unequal conditions, it seemed likely that they would feel things other than tenderness for one another: lack of understanding, prejudice, envy, even hatred. Tearing down the Wall wouldn't remove it. For it was the Wall alone that preserved the illusion that the Wall was the only thing separating the Germans.

I know almost no East Germans who escaped culture shock when they resettled in the West. Speaking a common language only highlighted their sense of being foreign, because it suggested a commonality that they did not experience day-to-day. I confess I often found it hard to understand their complaints. Something was always wrong. What can you say to the eternal criticisms that people in the West are "cold," that they "lack true friendship and solidarity," that "money isn't everything," that "life in the West is a rat race"? What did they expect? Didn't they know what they were getting into? Sometimes I had the sneaking suspicion that new arrivals from the East had unwittingly appropriated many of the "socialist virtues" that had been drummed into them. But these virtues seemed to blossom only in the West. No matter how loudly a new arrival proclaimed his anticommunism, after two glasses of vodka he would start dreaming about being "back home" where friends kept their word and the phrase "I'll be in touch" was more than just a phrase.

But how fundamental were these acquired differences? Were they superficial, or did they run so deep that they affected the traditions all Germans shared, their language, their view of history, their values? Were they sufficiently pronounced to sustain two separate German states without a Wall?

It took the events of September and October to shake (and shake up) the established configurations. Faced with television footage of East German refugees at the embassies in Prague and Budapest, of crowded trains rolling out of East and into West Germany, of unending columns of Trabants backed up at the border—faced with all this, even the staunchest supporters of the status quo had to concede that the politics of gradualism were over. A new type of refugee, hitherto unknown on such a vast scale, had stepped onto the stage of history: the prosperous refugee. Because these were not the wretched of the earth, these people arriving with a child on one arm and a plastic bag on the other. Most of them left behind a job, a three-room apartment, a TV set, and a car. Now they were standing in line to move from what was supposedly the tenth-wealthiest economy in the world to the third-wealthiest. Were they economic refugees? Of course they were, but that doesn't fully describe the phenomenon. The more intangible things they hoped to gain by giving up so much and crossing the border struck West Germans as strangely romantic: freedom, dignity, the right to live your life as you pleased. Such declarations reminded Western leftists of right-wing propaganda, and rightists of campaign slogans that had been worn to death. What were these people talking about? Did they know no more about the West than the commercials on TV? And did they really take them seriously?

This revealed a cultural gap as wide as the Wall was high: people who lack basic freedoms don't have to think very hard to name them, while people who enjoy them usually find it difficult to perceive their concrete value—from which it follows that when people claim they don't know what high-sounding notions like "human rights" really mean, you can be pretty certain they already have those rights.

November 9, 1989; Hanover, New Hampshire. I was sitting in the German Department at Dartmouth College gathering a few observations and musings under the title "What If the Wall Came Tumbling Down" for a French newspaper when someone burst in with news that the Wall had fallen. Impossible to sort out the tangle of feelings the news created in me. But right at the top, and with absolute clarity: I don't believe it, it can't be, not so fast and not so easy! How can they dispose of that concrete thing? And by the stroke of a pen—was there even a stroke of the pen? Maybe just a couple of words at a press conference? For the past twenty-eight years, that tyrant presence set the course of German, European, and even world history. Is it really now nothing more than a hundred-mile heap of dusty white cement? Only a dictatorship—which in this case had its good points—could undertake such crucial changes on the spur of the moment and without the slightest regard for diplomacy. It would have taken months to reach a similar decision in West Germany.

After the amazement and incomprehension came rejoicing. A political miracle had just occurred—it was like a child's Christmas, and no one could take the gift away. Only, who was the Santa Claus, whose gift was it, and what was really inside all the wrapping? In any case, it was a gift that brought joy to those immediately affected, regardless of the consequences. How could Germans feel anything but joy when the Wall—a monstrosity from the very start—finally came down—and peacefully? Whatever conflicts now appeared at the opened door, the new situation seemed infinitely better than the old. I wanted to buy champagne, celebrate, call friends, get on the plane—I really wanted to be there. I wanted to know more, and in more detail than American TV was able to tell me: Who are those people dancing on the Wall, toasting one another with bottles of champagne? Are they mostly East Berliners, or are West Berliners celebrating too? They've been dressing alike for a long time now, but what they feel underneath their leather and denim jackets must set them apart, and probably will for a long time to come. Who are those people waving flags and singing Deutschland über Alles? Who are those people singing the Internationale—are East Berlin teenagers singing along? Who are those people hammering away at the Wall like so many Sisyphuses, breaking it into pieces no bigger than gemstones? How many of my leftist friends are hammering alongside them, how many are sitting at home, appalled, delighted, and resolved not to succumb to this new outburst of German mania?

Other questions surfaced, questions about my future life in Berlin: Which bar in East Berlin will become my hangout? How long will it take for them to start serving Orvieto? And then: Now that it's going to get even more crowded in West Berlin, what's going to happen to the rents? How do the Turks, the Tamils, the Pakistanis feel about this German flood from the East? Won't a lot of them think that these all-too-white Germans are going to flip out again, that it's time to move on? The new arrivals will undoubtedly develop a very clear pecking order, with the East Germans at the top of the ladder, the ethnic Germans from Poland, Hungary, Romania, the Soviet Union down below, and the "non-German" foreigners on the very bottom rung. And these lowest of the low will hear more often than they ever heard before: "What are you doing here? Go home! We Germans have enough of our own problems!" Protecting—and expanding—the rights of these foreigners will be the most urgent task facing all Germans with any sense of history.

The opening of the Wall initially generated more confusion than clarity. When I saw President Bush comment on the historic event with sullen enthusiasm, I had the impression he was about to blurt out to his advisors: "Well, gentlemen, how am I supposed to feel about this?" It's worth asking what caused this confusion. A review of the three decades preceding November 9,

1989, suggests the following: the world—and this is particularly true of the world west of the Wall—the world had pondered the possibility of war more than the possibility of peace. No one had worked out a scenario for what had overnight become reality: life in Europe without the Wall. Moreover, the much-touted "resolution" of the German Question, the "unification of Europe," had for the moment been taken out of the politicians' hands. Once the new era had been ushered in by the Soviet policy of non-intervention, the pace and course of the peaceful revolution were set almost exclusively by the people behind the Wall who hitherto had been deprived of any voice. Only days after being forced to turn out in celebration of the Party, hundreds of thousands paraded in the streets of Leipzig, Dresden, and Berlin chanting, "We are the people." They confounded every schedule and forced regimes East and West to react, not act.

I'd like to say a word here for the East German citizens who, although scorned by many, played a pioneering role by seeking their well-being in mass flight to the West rather than in reform. I will confess that even I preferred East Germans who chose to stay put, though I suspected myself and everyone else who talked like that of selfish motives: it seemed clear that the ones who stayed put would cause us fewer problems than the ones who came. But looking back, I have to admit that without the columns of Trabants, without the tens of thousands of people whose mass departure made a sham of East Germany's fortieth-anniversary celebration, the opposition in East Germany could not have become such a popular movement.

The immediate and long-range questions posed by life without the Wall will require decades to answer: How will we communicate with each other now that our conversation is no longer distorted and disrupted by a wall? Where shall Germany belong—to the West, to the East, or somewhere in between? Will the very notion of "East" and "West" still have any meaning? But most of all: Can we exist without an enemy?

East–West Passages

In the days after the opening of the Wall, East Germany's national emblem underwent a remarkable transformation. The hammer and sickle vanished from the flag, leaving only a round hole in its stead, and reappeared in a slightly vulgarized form, as the hammer and chisel in the hands of thousands of Berliners (East and West) and tourists who began hacking away at the Wall. For weeks they attacked it, all along its hundred miles. Even from a distance you could hear them beating on its suddenly vulnerable surface, day in, day out; nothing, neither subzero temperatures nor steady rain nor dark of night, could keep the Wall-peckers away. They used whatever they could lay their hands on: some slugged at sharpened rods with the back of an ax, others used dainty hammers to tap on tiny screwdrivers that quickly broke. Some impromptu workers were even seen thrashing away with pocketknives. Few people had the proper tools, and the hardware stores soon ran out of chisels.

After November 9, you could tell Berliners by their swollen knuckles and blackened thumbnails.

This international brigade worked around the clock. It comprised people of all ages bound by a common noise and a common purpose: they came to destroy, not to build. Such harmony must have been heard in Babel before an angry God punished the presumptuous tower-builders by confusing their tongues. Individual incentive fostered the collective enterprise of destruction, as people everywhere succumbed to concrete fever. Bits of rubble that you could find on any construction site were passed on to eager customers like jewels, and at night, collectors combed the ground with flashlights and tweezers for the tiniest crumbs of painted cement.

At first glance, the price of a piece of Wall bore no reasonable relation to supply. Depending on size and coloring, a piece could run anywhere from three to seventy marks. Set in a "Wall brooch," the same piece could easily cost three times as much at a jewelry store. At one point, the going rate for Wall-prospectors was 150 marks an hour. Men and women in fur coats who had recently invested in paintings by Penck and Salomé now strolled among the vendors, picking out the nicest samples with a connoisseur's eye. Demand was especially high for specimens with bits of lettering on a painted background. Rumors spread of stockpiling. There was no telling when concrete from the Berlin Wall would reach parity with gold, but surely, once the Japanese got into the act . . . Only the East Germans sold cheap, unaccustomed as they were to the free market, slow to understand that the price of a commodity is determined by demand. Naturally, some of their Western competitors suspected them of shoddy business practices rather than naïveté, and accused them of dumping. By the Wall, with the Wall, and for a profit, the free market was running wild.

Wall work was more demanding than you might expect—people had underestimated the toughness of the Wall. In West Berlin, rumor had it that an American specialist in Oklahoma City had finally discovered that the Wall's diamond-like hardness was due to its high asbestos content. Members of the Green coalition, who had never complained about the Wall before, were suddenly decrying an "environmental scandal." One spokesperson recommended "breaking off breaking down the Wall," and proposed an "organized clean-up operation."

All of which raised the issue of ownership, because the longest and most famous—though not the most attractive—monument in East Germany belonged to the socialist state. The West only contributed the murals and graffiti. From the start, some voices in East Germany clamored to redirect the unbridled dismantling of the Wall in a planned way. An East Berlin company calling itself Export Wallworks was hastily organized, and soon announced the "sale of original pieces worldwide." All proceeds, the company said, would go to support humanitarian causes and public health care in East Germany. Border guards and traffic police would handle the dismantling and storage of pieces of the Wall. It smacked of a planned—i.e., unsuccessful—economy all over again. The best thing would probably have been to "privatize" the whole site and make it East Germany's first big business. But then again, what business could possibly protect such an asset from embezzlers and other, well, chiselers? Rockefeller and Trump knew what they were doing when they built skyward. So instead of being auctioned at Sotheby's, the Wall was unceremoniously peddled on black markets from Los Angeles to Istanbul.

You could almost feel sorry for the Wall. No one really wanted it. The watchtowers were empty; the few border police who remained at the Brandenburg Gate scrambled around with about as much respect for the Wall as tourists from the West, shooting pictures for the family album; the 5,000-plus police dogs who had "patrolled" it were placed in animal shelters to await new masters. Like a totem deconsecrated, divested of its power and felled to the ground, it lay there, a monstrous absurdity, while the fantasies of triumph and freedom once painted on it by those it kept apart fell away letter by letter. By the end of the year, nothing remained of this mythic defender of the status quo, nothing but some stretches of gray wall with the wind blowing through the holes.

As I said, the day they opened the Wall, I was at Dartmouth brooding over an article about what would happen if the Wall fell. The news that made the hypothesis real reached me about 2:30 P.M. local time. I logged off the computer and called a friend in West Berlin. He didn't believe me. True, the seven o'clock news from the East had featured someone named Schabowski impassively reading something about the checkpoints being open, but no one took it seriously. However, since I was calling from overseas, he promised to go out and take a look.

When I came home four weeks later, I felt the best way to make up for not having been there was to ask everyone I met what they had experienced that November 9.

The Berlin cabbie who drove me home from Tegel Airport hadn't been to East Berlin since the Wall went up. Incredibly, he just happened to schedule his first visit for the evening of the ninth: for two weeks he'd been carrying a ticket in his wallet to *Simply Charming*, a musical revue at the Friedrichstadt Palace. According to him, everything seemed normal until the intermission. During the second half he was disturbed by loud whispering and shuffling in the aisles. But he wasn't really upset until the spectators began leaving the theater in droves. At first he thought the place was on fire. But since there wasn't any smoke, and since no one seemed to be fleeing the theater in a panic, he assumed the audience was just unimpressed, which struck him as unfair: the girls were terrific, you couldn't see a better cancan in Paris. It was just before the end of the show that he heard about the Wall being opened, but he didn't see this as a reason to leave. He hadn't been to the theater in twenty-eight years, and he was determined to stay through the evening. By the last number, he was one of about two dozen people left in the enormous hall; the girls on stage seemed grateful for the few devoted customers—it seemed to him they were kicking their legs a little higher. But he also had the impression that several pairs of legs were missing on stage. Later, crossing back to the West, he got caught in a huge Trabant-jam, and couldn't understand what everyone was so ecstatic about. He remembered all too well working on a construction site in the days before August 13, 1961, and his foreman's threat, "If you don't get moving, I'll bring someone in from over there who'll do it for half the price!"

A Trabant driver from East Berlin remembered November 9 mostly as a traffic nightmare. He heard about the opening of the "ramparts" while working on the night shift. Like most of his colleagues, he tore off his work clothes and left to see for himself. He went straight home, got his wife and children out of bed, and set out with the whole family on a night ride to the West. "I've never been so scared in my entire life!" he said. "Just the way they welcomed us—pounding on the roof of the car! People in the West don't know how thin a Trabi is, it isn't made of steel, you know, it's plastic mixed with cotton, and when you're inside, you wonder if the car is going to hold up! And the people! They were like locusts, they practically threw themselves against the windshield, you couldn't get rid of them! My wife was driving blind, with her face right up against the glass, and I just sat there and shook. And the rules of the road on your side— they just don't make sense. It's ridiculous to have the right of way when you're coming out of a little side street onto a main avenue. The little ones ahead of the big ones—you'll have to straighten that out! So we drove around for a while and then went back, and were we happy to get home again. At least here you know what you're doing wrong!"

A Greek bartender I know saw an East Berlin family waiting in line for a peep show on Joachimsthaler Strasse. The wife was holding her two teenage daughters by the hand: "Come on, let your father get his kicks for once, we'll just wait over here!" The solidarity of this East German nuclear family impressed my Mediterranean friend. What husband in the West, he asked, could count on that kind of understanding?

Another mother was standing in front of KaDeWe (Kaufhaus des Westens, West Berlin's leading department store) with her two kids, all dressed in standard-issue, stone-washed jeans. "Okay, now," she said, "we're going in. Just act normal!"

D., a teacher in a daycare center, didn't catch the evening news on the ninth. The next morning, in the subway on her way to work, she was surprised by the crowds, and especially by the number of denim jackets. She told me she remembered thinking, "Those people look like they're from the East!" As she was opening the daycare center at about 8:00 A.M., she had a close encounter of the third kind. Two Trabants came racing down the street beeping their horns and screeched to a halt. Eight strapping teenagers struggled out of the Lilliputian cars, sprayed champagne all around, hugged some of the children—whom they had never seen in their lives and who

were scared to death—lifted them up, and danced with
them in the street.

A not-quite-so-young couple from Berlin-Wilmersdorf
spent the evening of November 9 in bed with the TV
on. During a break in their lovemaking, they happened
to hear a reporter on "News Today" asking Helmut Kohl
whether he wouldn't rather be in Berlin than in Warsaw
just then. The chancellor's response got lost in the male
partner's tender attentions. The chancellor, already famous for his clumsiness, had recently distinguished himself by consistently showing up precisely where nothing
was happening. In any case, the reporter's question kept
gnawing at the female partner's brain, although it wasn't
at its most receptive: if the chancellor's absence, this
time from Berlin, was once again making news, it was a
sure sign that history had visited the divided city that
day. What Helmut Kohl was missing in Warsaw, the
passionate couple had missed in their king-size bed.
When the woman stepped out on her balcony the next
morning and inhaled the unusually strong scent of East
German gasoline, she understood in a flash what the
reporter had meant: "I could smell it!"

The vegetable lady across the way has a friend who lives
in a single-family house right by the Berlin-Staaken
checkpoint. Shortly before midnight on November 9, he
felt the urge to give his greenhouse one last look. On
his way out, he discovered an unceasing flow of people,
yelling and swinging bottles as they passed through the
normally deserted checkpoint. In the crowd, a strange

apparition drew his gaze: a woman was tiptoeing past the customhouse in her nightgown, as self-assured as if she were sleepwalking. Then, suddenly, she stopped and began searching the ground.

"Where's the line?"

"What do you mean, *line?*" the vegetable grower asked.

"Am I in the West now?"

"I think so. But take a few more steps if you want to be absolutely sure!"

"I can't believe there isn't a line here somewhere! How can I be sure I'm really in the West now?"

"If you want to be absolutely positive, come into my house and have a glass of champagne!"

"No thanks, this is enough for now, I'll come back tomorrow when I'm dressed." And with that the apparition extended a slipper over an invisible line, performed a pirouette, and floated back to the East.

Some West Berliners with whom I spoke were reminded of stories about the day the Aztecs met the Spaniards, though that left unclear who the Indians were this time around. For others, it was E.T. coming to Earth; this analogy broke down quickly too, though, because of the number of aliens involved. Most were surprised at how deeply the encounter moved them. Of course, it was those coming through the forbidden door to the West for the first time who set off the happy frenzy. But West Berliners got carried away, too, and wept tears of joy. The western half of the city gave the visitors from the eastern half an unprecedented welcome party.

It wasn't just the mainstream that was flooded by this vast feeling of community. Even hard-core leftists who believed themselves immune to such sentiments weakened that night, and still reeling weeks later, confessed to me that they, too, had shed tears. When I asked what exactly had brought on these surprising secretions, I learned it had nothing to do, thank God, with nationalist feeling, nor even with long-suppressed family feeling, nor with a longing for reunification. It was something much simpler, much more universal: "Those people had been locked in for so long, and suddenly they were out. You should have seen the way they came through, the way they stared at everything! It really got to you!" A little later, this speaker, obviously embarrassed he had let his emotions get the better of him, added, "If you ask me, reunification already took place on November 9, but I don't like it!"

The opening of the Wall had clearly challenged long-held positions and unleashed new feelings that cannot be reduced to the common denominator of "Germany," feelings at once more modest and more generous than the "new nationalism" presumptuously cited by campaigning politicians. A wall that opens after three decades is a universal metaphor of great power. Among the many grotesque miscalculations of East Germany's rulers, none was greater than the decision to protect the "Socialist Fatherland" by constructing an edifice that was bound to evoke a yearning for freedom in men and women everywhere. In building the Wall, they instantly generated worldwide sympathy for the Germans—not exactly everyone's darlings—and the German Question.

Had they erected a structure less charged with symbol-ism, neither the Germans nor their "problem" would have touched the hearts of mankind in quite the same way.

In truth, the East German Wall-builders were only casting in concrete a "misconception" that originated with the victors of World War II. If the Allies had really meant to achieve a long-term partition, and if they had known German history, they would never have drawn a line from north to south: it would have run west to east. Had they separated Baden-Württemberg, Bavaria, and even Saxony from the "Prussian North" with a medium-width, minimally landscaped trench, they could have relied on historical fault lines and likely enlisted the aid of a good part of the population. Instead, they drew a totally artificial and arbitrary border separating West and East that was doomed from the start.

My November 9 was made possible by Tom Brokaw and NBC, whose great camera angles made up for the less-than-insightful commentary. The images of Berliners re-joicing and dancing on the Wall overwhelmed me, and not just because I live in Berlin. I saw them making a mass sport out of an activity I had described eight years earlier in *The Wall Jumper*, an activity then practiced by only a few isolated oddballs. The scenes from No-vember 9 revealed the simple motivation behind my heroes' often whimsical and mysterious behavior: from the beginning, their goal had been to avoid crossing the border legally, to refuse to recognize the border at all; now everyone was doing it, and on top of the Wall itself people celebrated the collapse of one of the wonders of the postwar world. There was one startling technical detail: many people could be seen climbing up on the Wall, but none were seen falling down. One of that night's many discoveries must have been that, in the security zone by the Brandenburg Gate, the Wall is as wide as a disco dance floor. And the most glorious, unforgettable image was the cyclist who pedaled along the Wall until he vanished into the distance off the screen.

Television may well be an "empty" medium. But for the sake of accuracy, it ought to be added that it is an empty medium with the power to shape history. No verbal report, however eloquent, could approach the emotional impact of the images from the Wall party. In the United States, where news from Germany normally gets a matter of seconds, the week-long TV spots of Berliners dancing on the Wall signaled a historic turning point: suddenly, positively, and decisively they changed the German public image. Of course, the standard documentaries—in color—of industrious Germans and their economic miracle had generated a kind of bloodless respect, but they could never seriously compete with the black-and-white pictures of Nazis extending their arms in the Hitler salute. November 9 was perhaps the first time since the war that the Germans met with worldwide sympathy: people were amazed that Germans were capable of having a good time.

These new images of Berlin finally had the power to act as an emotional counterweight. The hated Nazi German and the boring but respected economic miracle-worker German were now joined by a new figure: the warm, likable German. After the president of the United States gave the historic event a rather cool nod during a press conference, he spent the next two days defending himself against American journalists who reproached him for not showing more feeling and enthusiasm. Secretary of State James Baker grew tired of the constant questioning and finally admitted to being "deeply moved," at the same time relating a phone call from Hans Dietrich Genscher, the German foreign minister, thanking him for the support of successive U.S. administrations. And I thought: For God's sake, how is it that the American secretary of state can't even appear on camera six thousand miles away without feeling obliged to shed a tear of emotion?

No one should be misled, though: the new sympathy for Germany has no permanent worldwide guarantee. The postwar era may have ended, but Germany's crimes will remain vivid in the minds of the victims for centuries to come, a point that was missed at the official festivities following the impromptu parties. No German politician stated explicitly that this Wall now being "dismantled by the people" (Mayor Momper) had not been some tragic injustice, but the direct result of a world war the Germans had begun, or that its destruction awakened memories of German guilt worldwide. And just after November 9, T-shirts proclaiming NOV. 9—I WAS THERE! were being sold at a kiosk on Potsdamer Platz. Only Richard Chaim Schneider, the son of a Holocaust survivor, was struck by how much forgetfulness was required to achieve the new exultation. "I was breathless at the sight of this T-shirt," he wrote in *Die Zeit* (December 29). "What was happening? Were the Germans suddenly admitting they'd been there? On November 9, 1938? On Kristallnacht?"

Charles Bukowski begins one of his stories with the line, "The first three months of my marriage to Sarah were acceptable, but I'd say a little after that our troubles began."

Scene in a West Berlin disco, December 1989.

"Give me the key!"

"You've got your own!"

"But it's my apartment."

"So what—does that mean I'm supposed to sleep in the East again from now on?"

"What do I care! I just don't want someone coming over all the time without telling me!"

The opening of the Wall spelled catastrophe for a lot of people who had based their happiness on the structure's durability. The West Berlin woman demanding her key back was no longer so enamored of her East Berlin lover once he could come over and see her anytime. And things got even more complicated. West Berlin Romeos, including a good number of Turks, had supplemented their marriages in the West with romantic attachments in the East, which the Wall had kept in a constant state of pleasant high tragedy. On the long night of November 9, and into the gray morning of the tenth, not a few voyagers from the East stood unannounced at doors in the West, while the offspring they had in hand cheerily called, "Hi, Daddy, so this is where you live!"

Even a happily married Berlin couple—he German,

she Polish, with two children—suddenly confronted domestic problems that could only be attributed to November 9. The woman felt threatened by the new Germans from the East: "These people haven't known a day of democracy in fifty years, and, what's more, they've inherited the Nazis' hatred of the Poles almost undiluted."

He: "So, do you want to leave?"

She: "I've been thinking about packing my bags ever since all these Germans with clear consciences began showing up."

He: "But this is the first time I've ever really enjoyed Berlin!"

When I got back, four weeks after the big day, I found the city surprisingly unchanged. No sign of the knee-deep banana peels people had supposedly waded through for days in Wilmersdorfer Strasse. The chocolate Easter bunnies that appeared in bakeries when chocolate Santa Clauses sold out—maybe that was a joke after all. The stories about West Berliners having to do their weekend shopping by noon on Thursday because the shelves were empty after that—so far as I could tell, a rumor. The much-deplored overnight transformation of West Berlin, after the East German invasion, into a derelict city that looked hopelessly like East Berlin—not true either, though perhaps an accurate forecast.

The more privileged natives quickly found a way to get along. "You just change your habits: you shop at Butter Lindner instead of Bolle," one observer explained laconically. "The coffee costs two marks more, but at least you don't have to stand in line!" A few took taxis out to Dahlem, a neighborhood of villas, to shop at the local Aldi (discount) market. And in the elegant cafés around Savignyplatz, where an appetizer costs twelve marks, November 9 never happened at all. "There was a bigger crowd for the film festival," one owner remarked.

Only in front of super-discount stores, electronics shops, and post offices (where every East German could receive 100 marks of "welcome money" until year's end) did I encounter the fabled triple-loop lines. In Wilmersdorf, in a pedestrian mall with shops catering to the not-so-well-to-do, a lot of things suddenly cost much, much more: Walkmen, radios with cassette decks, cameras, ski jackets, and, of course, the standard-issue blue jeans.

It seems there was absolutely no need for the writer Heiner Müller to encourage his countrymen—as he did in *Der Spiegel*—to clean out KaDeWe instead of squashing their noses against the display windows. At the big Hertie store, a new announcement boomed over the loudspeaker: "Please watch your handbags!" The police reported that the number of break-ins and thefts doubled during the last two weeks of November. A life-and-death struggle for space erupted precisely where there was no room to spare, where poor met poor: at the housing and welfare agencies, and in residential neighborhoods where people still used coal heat and the toilet was on the landing. That's where those who couldn't afford the new elation said out loud what they didn't like about the Wall—it wasn't impermeable any more.

The first time I cross the border, I notice they've removed the pictures of Erich Honecker from the customs buildings. The pale rectangle on the wall has stayed empty. Could it possibly be the same size as the space another dictator left famously empty on German walls after May 1945? I ask the border official when they took down the general secretary. Two days after his resignation, he tells me. And who'll fill the spot now? He shrugs, grins: "Good question." The border official's friendliness, laxness even, seems eerie. The harsh voice is still ringing in my ears, I'm still waiting for that inexorable gaze fixed on the bridge of my nose as the seconds tick by. Instead he waves me through, jokes, asks me with genuine interest when I plan to visit again! Nothing about the border makes sense anymore: a friend of mine went over on her daughter's passport and didn't notice her mistake until she was sitting at a café in East Berlin. From the vantage of the present, the border experiences of the past twenty years seem like a hallucination: Was it all just a bad dream? Can habits so long ingrained be so quickly broken? What went on in these people's heads when the Wall fell, the Wall that gave them their power and position for so many years? What did they do with the fear, the bewilderment, the sense of betrayal?

"What did you do on November 9?" I asked.

"I went to work. After all, we were the ones who had to deal with the confusion."

"Were you happy? I mean you personally?"
"Well, why shouldn't I be? I'm not complaining. Have
a good trip!"
Why did I wish he had refused to answer?

It isn't until I walk around the city that I discover what
I could have gathered from any map. Although I've
known West Berlin's Potsdamer Platz for years, only now
do I realize it leads directly through a hole in the Wall
to East Berlin's Leipziger Strasse, which I've also known
for years. By going through the Brandenburg Gate,
which until recently marked the end of the Western
world, you arrive at Berlin Center and Pariser Platz, and
just beyond that is Unter den Linden. In Berlin, what
people were calling "wild," "crazy," "incredible," was in
truth the most normal thing in the world: the ability to
walk from one end of the street to the other. Having
grown accustomed to an insane situation, we experienced
normalization as crazy. For instance, although they had
always been visible, this is the first time I actually use
the buildings in the West that stand higher than the Wall
to orient myself in East Berlin. To go back, I just head
toward the Reichstag—it's suddenly that simple.

But there was something missing during this first, and
later during my second and third visits: What was I looking for? Gaiety, defiance, triumph, a touch of euphoria—
of the restrained and moderate German kind of course—
and even a little well-deserved pride. After all, wasn't
this the first successful and, what's more, peaceful revolution in Germany, the one Karl Marx had always hoped

for and anticipated—though this time, ironically, it entailed a victory against socialism?

The four construction workers I met at the Sports Corner, a bar in Prenzlauer Berg (East Berlin), were already pretty well drunk by four in the afternoon. No one seemed particularly interested in conversation. "Open the Wall, close the Wall, what's it going to change for us," one of them said. "Business is so bad here that anyone from the West who invested in it would lose his shirt. The SED [Socialist Unity Party] is talking about a sellout. I wish we could. Because if you sell out, it means someone's buying."

In parting, he offered to sell me a party medal for five marks: "My boss awarded it to me this morning." I bought it on approval. "If you can get rid of the damned thing for ten marks in the West, we can start dealing in Communist decorations. Talk about unlimited supply!"

Later, I went to a press conference called by the United Left in the Information Center on Alexanderplatz. Bettina Wegner, a once-proud protest singer driven from East Germany about ten years ago, was playing a mellow guitar—tonic, dominant, subdominant—and to the applause of a mildly bewildered audience sang the following confession about her departure (my memory may be a bit polemical here):

> I gave no one away, I did nothing wrong,
> I was just too scared to hang on till the fall.

But maybe I should only hum this song,
And maybe in time stop playing at all.

After that I went on to the special convention of the
Socialist Unity Party at the Dynamo Sports Hall. The
large number of guards in the corridors of the enormous gymnasium was striking; they practically outnum-
bered the delegates. You couldn't go to the bathroom,
let alone get something to eat, without flashing one of
the various press cards. In the auditorium, nearly every
speaker obediently parroted the same idea: "This is a
burden we simply have to bear!" The question what
burden they were talking about got submerged in dutiful
applause. After giving the pledge-and-evasion line, they
inevitably proceeded to distinguish between themselves
and the "criminals." It seems that, following the Chinese
model, a gang of four misled the rank and file: Honecker,
Mielke, Hager—and who was the fourth one? Since
everyone, including the audience, could think of a million names to add here, they preferred to applaud. No
one made the simple statement that also didn't get said
forty-five years before: "Comrades! I played along. I believed in it, believed in them. And now I'm shaken,
speechless. Please, don't let me forget that I have nothing
to say, not now, and not in years to come."
Instead of disbanding, instead of surrendering their
ill-gotten gains and shutting their mouths, the Socialist
Unity Party simply mounted the next-biggest pony with
any life left in it. This new horse is called democratic
socialism, and has the advantage of never having run a
race.

The pundits west of the Wall also hurried to adjust their earlier declarations, prognoses, and options. They talked as though the events were simply a pleasant surprise, as though nothing significant had happened. Why is it so hard to admit to mistakes in this country? Instead, Germans on both sides seem intent on proving that this revolution—which happened in spite of them—was something they had always desired and predicted.

At the flea market on Potsdamer Platz, I asked a Turk what the opening of the Wall meant to him. "Wonderful!" he said. "I was thrilled!" But wouldn't he face increasing competition? "Wonderful, no problem!" he repeated, and laughed. I felt as if he had caught me trying to justify my own worldview by making people confess to problems they didn't really have. It was only when he delivered the table I'd bought from him that I discovered that customers like me get different answers before and after a sale. He hadn't wanted to drive off a potential German buyer by answering too openly. "We're all scared," he said over a cup of coffee. "At noon today, the Pole who works two stands down had all four tires on his car slashed. While we were trying to fix them, two other Poles came along who had had the same thing happen to them. So far, we Turks are better off. We've been living here for thirty years now, we know the language and don't run around with our faces stuck in a map. But how long will our good fortune last?"

"I was three years old when we came here, I grew up here," said his wife, who had come along. "I'm not German, but I'm not a foreigner either. What kind of a place is this that they still treat you like a foreigner when you've been here thirty years. The only thing that sets me apart from the Germans is that I don't look German. What's so terrible about that?"

It's true: they're Germanizing West Berlin now, and the words on the Wall—PLEASE, DON'T LEAVE US ALONE WITH THE GERMANS!—have probably long since fallen to the chisel. The Germans now coming in from the East aren't used to anything non-German. Foreigners make up 12 percent of West Berlin's population, while in the whole of East Germany they constituted barely 1 percent.

For some time now, people have been talking in the West German media about a "multicultural" society. I believe the Germans from the East have good and very personal reasons for joining in this discussion. Once the initial euphoria over unification subsides, it will become painfully clear that not only did two states spring up on either side of the Wall, but two cultures as well, and two different ways of life. We can't yet say how much of each will disappear and how much will survive. For now, one thing is certain: our neighbors aren't the only ones who need to fear a unification that may wipe out every difference.

• • • • •

Sentimental Germany

In mid-November of 1989, television audiences around the world stared in shock at a banner held aloft in a tiny village. It bore the following phrase in clumsily written letters: HELMUT, YOU'RE OUR CHANCELLOR TOO!

This bold address was something of an embarrassment to West Germany's chancellor, though he had recently taken a liking to being called by his first name. For the banner wasn't raised in Leipzig or in Dresden, but in Poland—to be precise, in the hamlet of Krzyżowa, Kreisau to Germans—during Helmut Kohl's visit there. In Krzyżowa (population 100), cows and hens bid each other good night by the light of the moon; now, thanks to that banner, the tiny hamlet suddenly found itself in the spotlight of the world press. For a short time, Krzyżowa focused all the fears that neighboring peoples harbor about German unification: Once they're all gathered under one roof, won't the Germans get greedy and start eyeing all the territories they've lost?

The matter didn't end with the alarm sounded in Krzyżowa. As the Soviet empire collapsed, German minorities everywhere across the continent began to stir, although both their fatherlands had nearly forgotten them. In the Soviet Union, the Volga Germans demanded autonomy; in far-off Romania, well over 100,000 ethnic Germans announced their wish to emigrate; and in French Alsace, the German minority, taking their cue from the East, argued the "advance of bilingualism." People were suddenly speaking German again—out loud and without shame—from the left bank of the Rhine to the right bank of the Volga. The sound sent shock waves around the world.

It's worth asking what has surfaced here, forty-five years after the end of World War II. As a point of departure, let us take the most sensitive and provocative case—the German minority in Poland. Even half-enlightened Germans shudder at the mention of their brethren next door, for the issue of the "Silesian Germans" inevitably calls to mind Germany's right-wing Silesian Patriots' Club and the League of Deportees, the umbrella organization representing Germans who were forced to leave Poland and Czechoslovakia after World War II. Some twelve million Germans were expelled, and the League claims a membership of 2.3 million. Not long ago, the League's president, Herbert Czaja, attacked the chancellor of the Federal Republic for voting to confirm the Oder-Neisse line as Poland's western border. How, Czaja asked, could the head of state "surrender 41,000 square miles of Germany" without violating his oath of office? Later statements only provided further proof of Czaja's extreme position: the man really does want most, if not all, of Silesia back. But incorrigible as he is, did Czaja speak in any way for the Germans of Poland?

I decided to drive to Krzyżowa to find out who had raised that troublesome banner, and what they were after. I thought all I needed for my project was a car and a good map, but it wasn't that easy. Krzyżowa was not to be found—neither on my map of Poland nor in German guidebooks to the area. My mental preparations for the trip confronted me with even bigger problems. I've never been strong on German folkways, and I'm no fan of zither playing. The mere idea of spending a week with the founders of German men's choirs and the avant-garde of folk costume groups brought on a hangover that normally requires at least two bottles of Baden white wine.

I began my research by visiting German Red Cross reception centers in West Berlin, where East Germans and ethnic Germans from Poland await living quarters and a job in their new homeland. As it happens, though, I learned nothing here I didn't already know about the Germans in Poland. With one exception, none of the Poles I met spoke any German, and no one had heard of a village called Krzyżowa. When I asked them about their place of origin, it's true most of them did make a visible effort to give German names for towns that now are Polish: names like Hindenburg, Seydlitzruh, Heinrichau. They probably felt this was the price of admission to their host country. After that, all conversation died. Language wasn't the problem—I'd arranged for an interpreter—but my topic was. The Poles simply feared they might raise doubts about their Germanness by revealing too much information. The standard response to my question as to why they were emigrating was: Believe me, I didn't do it for economic reasons. Then why? Discrimination at home? A love affair with the German soul? One Polish woman proclaimed it was just that she liked everything about Germany—German houses, the leaves on German trees, German streets, the green of German parks.

The Poles are pushed to such degrading convolutions as a result of the German immigration regulations previously mentioned. If ethnic Germans from Poland have no German parent or grandparent in their family tree, they must in effect prove that their parents or grandparents "committed" themselves to Germanity. Such commitment can be deduced from a parent's or grandparent's inscription in section 3 of the People's Register. The Nazis established the Register in 1939, principally for the purpose of conscripting Polish citizens for service in the German army. For the Nazis, Poles who allowed their names to be inscribed in the Register—usually under duress—were considered "Germanizable" or "German on approval." About 90 percent of the Poles who now apply to immigrate base their petition on the People's Register. Practically speaking, then, the Pole who presents his father's or his grandfather's National Socialist German Workers' Party card acquires all the privileges of a German citizen, while a compatriot whose father or grandfather died in the Warsaw Uprising against the Nazi barbarians has no case for asylum.

It is scandalous that even today the authorities allow

themselves to be guided by the Nazis' passion for Germanity. Such an immigration policy is simply another form of Aryanism—how else can one understand the ranking of petitioners according to their degree of "Germanness"? The alternative, of course, would be a quota system assuring all Poles an equal right to admission, regardless of how much German blood they have. Still, I hesitate to argue for eliminating the Register, since, by a quirk of history, this relic of the blood-and-soil era guarantees well over 100,000 "pure-blooded" Poles a year the right to settle in Germany with all the privileges of citizenship.

The legally sanctioned contest over who is more German is fought daily in the corridors of the reception centers. Many of the East Germans—who don't hesitate to identify themselves as economic refugees—view the Polish immigrants as second-class Germans who don't really belong. You hear comments like: "Some get in just because their grandmother had a German shepherd." A German-speaking Pole from Zabrze (formerly Hindenburg) responded to a question about relations between East Germans and Poles at the reception center this way: "I haven't had any trouble. I stay on my floor and don't talk with the Germans."

Curiously, a similar competition also occurs among the East Germans. What matters is how much you suffered to get to the West. Those who submitted their petition to emigrate two or three years earlier look down on the newcomers who waltzed over after November 9. "They don't know what they're in for in the West," the veterans say. They even show disdain for those who poured into the West in the summer of 1989 through Hungary or the West German embassy in Prague. "They got themselves a suntan on the Plattensee and then, hippity-hop, they're in the West." An older man who struggled for two years to emigrate told me openly, "I don't think reunification's a good idea anymore, the ways things are now." Among the more respectable people in this hierarchy is an older couple whose tragic case moves even the new arrivals. The couple owned a lake house in Berlin-Friedrichshagen, as well as a sailboat and even a surfboard; they owed their prosperity to a private glassworks. The two had waited years to be allowed to emigrate, and had finally arrived in West Berlin just before November 9. For them, the opening of the Wall proved a disaster: it set off a marital crisis that resounded throughout the reception center. On November 9, it was all for nothing—the years of waiting, the arguments for and against, the sleepless nights, the crucial decision to leave and the pain of abandoning their house. Only one thing was certain: the man—now working as a window-washer in the West—would never even begin to approach his former standard of living. But the worst of it was that the two couldn't face the tragedy together. The wife drove her husband mad with plans to return. One month later, after she had calmed down, her husband succumbed to incurable homesickness; by then, of course, his wife was determined to stay. It went on like that for half a year; the couple couldn't stop fighting and finally had to see a psychiatrist for help.

♦

I find out that Krzyżowa, once Kreisau, lies not far from Wrocław, once Breslau. On my way there I stop in the Saxon city of Leipzig, which the writer Christoph Hein had proposed for the honorific designation of *Heldenstadt*, or City of Heroes, for it was there that the now legendary Monday demonstrations began the peaceful revolution in East Germany the previous October. On February 5, 1990, I join some 60,000 demonstrators in front of City Hall, and lose myself in a sea of black-red-gold flags. The flags of 1989 had a hole in the middle, suggesting an impaired, unfinished sense of identity, but they have apparently long since been replaced by unflawed versions. My suspicion that the new flags were brought in by West German political parties is met with angry denials. It seems the vast majority of the flags were made at home on East German sewing machines—the department stores had all sold out of black, red, and gold cloth. Twelve-year-old children are running around with their faces made up in the same three colors; a man well into his eighties carries a black-red-gold umbrella. The composition of the crowd has changed radically since October. Only a few placards display the wit and impertinence evident at the outset; one in particular deserves to be recorded for posterity: the bearded head of Karl Marx and the words WORKERS OF THE WORLD, FORGIVE ME!

It's evident that the young Christians, ecologists, and humanists of the New Forum who had set the protest in motion have decided to stay home. Only a few months have passed, and they can no longer recognize the baby they have brought into the world. In the meantime the streets have been taken over by the majority that preferred staying home in October and that now sees only one solution to all its problems: Germany! In all my fifty years, I've never heard that word chorused by live voices with so much fervor. "Wir sind ein Volk! Schwarz-Rot-Gold!" (We're all one Folk! Black-red-gold!) I recognize the tone of voice from archival footage shot before my birth. It's hard not to leap from comparison to equation. I'm disturbed—and that's as it should be. Yet to call this fascism would be misleading. A more helpful and mathematically accurate interpretation follows from the speeches delivered later at City Hall: for most of those present, "Germany" = deutsche marks − socialism. The Monday crowd in Leipzig sees unification as the only way out of forty years of misery.

Some distance away, a small group is flying a banner that reads DON'T THROW THE GDR AWAY! Eight young people cluster around a tiny East German flag, tensed for an attack. "Down with the red brood!" someone yells in their direction, and "Freedom, not socialism." A family man carrying a huge German flag in a holster across his belly wanders over to the group. "Stasi* brats," he shouts, "you've never worked a day in your life, you don't know what work is!"

The Monday crowd in Leipzig needed its scapegoats along the road to Germany. It seems that Manichaean

---

* Stasi: short for Staatssicherheitsdienst, the East German State Security Police.

worldviews are in the ascendant. At a time when the conservative press has once again discovered the worthlessness of intellectuals and the wisdom of the people, it seems a word about the people is in order. The simple truth is, the "people" have just as much reason to examine themselves as the intellectuals. The popular rage at the Socialist Unity Party, the Stasi, and the intellectuals also contains a lot of lapsed memory and probably some self-hatred as well, because the same majority now so vocal in its opposition was until recently just as silent in its obedience.

After the demonstration, discussion groups gather at the Menzel Fountain in front of City Hall. A tall young man in a trench coat, too well dressed to be a native, sets the tone. "It's time all Germans lived together again in one fatherland!"

"Including the ones on the other side of the Oder-Neisse line?" I ask.

"When you're talking twelve million deportees, I have trouble accepting the way things are."

"But, after all, it was Hitler who attacked the Poles, not the other way around!" a Leipzig man replies.

"We're not talking Hitler anymore, we're talking Germany," a young Saxon answers from the midst of a group consisting entirely of young males. "And if the Poles are going to ask Russia for what they lost in the East, why shouldn't we Germans also get back what rightly belongs to us?"

"What about the rights of twenty million dead Russians and their families?" another man from Leipzig asks.

"Yeah, but you're not a Russian, you're a Saxon," his neighbor reproaches him. They're still unsure of their arguments; forty years' worth of thoughts never stated, or at most confined to home, are now making their way into public in clumsy German. The vast majority of the group rejects the idea of adjusting Poland's western borders. But that doesn't stop the speaker in the trench coat.

His accent gives him away as a native of Hamburg. His arguments sound practiced and he delivers them well. He goes in for esoteric historical reasoning, a man with an idea: he mentions an English historian named Liddel Hart who has supposedly shown that the Germans have waged fewer wars than any other people . . .

I look into his precocious child's face with its blazing missionary gaze. The stereotype applies: blond hair, blue eyes, a white shirt and a snugly knotted tie. I can almost write off the dangerous stupidities being spouted by a few Leipzigers in defiance of forty years of educational dictatorship, but what is it that drives this son of the Hamburg middle class? The explanations I've heard for the new popularity of the *Republikaner*, a xenophobic right-wing party, don't fit. This kid doesn't belong to the neglected third of a three-tier society, he isn't on the waiting list for public housing, and he will not be satisfied by material comforts alone: he has a mission.

On the way to my hotel, I find thousands of leaflets the right-wingers had distributed that day in Leipzig, despite a ban. The torn-up leaflets litter the street. At least for the moment, the West's self-satisfied, ideologically motivated revanchism seems to have found little response in the East. But I can't help thinking that as unification puts millions of East Germans out of work, missionary zeal from the West, coupled with the pent-up frustration of disappointed D-mark patriots in the East, could produce a very explosive mix.

We push on to Poland, and Silesia. Culturally German for centuries, Silesia was given to Poland after World War I, fell to the Nazis in 1939, and reverted to Poland after World War II in compensation for the loss of its eastern provinces to the Soviet Union. Nearly all its Germans were forcibly repatriated to Allied-administered West Germany. Today, some 600,000 to 800,000 Polonized but ethnically German citizens still live in the region, almost all of them in Upper Silesia, its southern half. Germans have not had an easy time of it. Until January 1990, it was illegal to speak, read, or teach German in Upper Silesia. (Because there are so few Germans in Lower Silesia, its anti-German laws were relaxed in the 1950s.)

Crossing the border into Poland I exchange fifty D-marks for a little more than 300,000 zlotys, a Pole's average monthly income. The friend accompanying me grew up in Poland; she can't believe the exchange rate. Eight years ago, that sum still bought a car. Just like their neighbors, the Poles wound up in ruinous dependency on the Soviet empire as a result of German aggression; but they had no big brother bringing D-marks— instead, they count on vodka to make it through the day. In the small town near the border where we stop for lunch, I see a crowd of happy customers at the next table—all remarkably cheerful. When someone orders a beer, the waitress brings everyone two bottles apiece. No sooner has she turned away than they pull their own high-proof alcohol out of their briefcases and pour it into the beer glasses, which they then down quickly. Anyway, according to the papers, there's every reason to celebrate: there are more goods in the stores than at any time in the last forty years. Still, for now most Poles can only press their noses to the glass. It's true that everyone has a wad of bills as thick as a paving stone, and not one of the bills carries less than three figures—but that will barely buy a loaf of bread.

We reach Krzyżowa at dusk, only to discover it's the wrong Krzyżowa. After a glance at our license plates, the locals naturally know what we want. "Helmut, Helmut," they say tolerantly, and direct us toward a point on the horizon. "You want to go there, where your chancellor was." It is dark when we finally arrive at the site where Kohl made his appearance. The only light for miles around comes from the waning moon. Our ringing at the door of a church brings the sexton out of her miserable shack; she offers us a cup of tea. She describes what a shock it was for her, a Pole, when the Germans arrived. A rumor had been going around that the Germans were buying Count von Moltke's estate, and the village into the bargain: they planned to set up a German-Polish retreat here. She immediately assumed everyone would have to pull up stakes once again—"But the Germans are sure to give us land somewhere as compensation, aren't they?" Together with her girl friend, she had come to Krzyżowa from Poland's lost eastern provinces in 1945, as had pretty much everyone else here. There wasn't a single German either in Krzyżowa or in the neighboring villages; and as for the thousands of Germans who had turned out for Helmut Kohl's visit—well, they must have come from Upper Silesia, from East and even from West Germany.

She leads us through the darkness to the scene of the historic event. We enter a square, enclosed farmyard. The stables had been hastily whitewashed—on one side only—and from the gloom, a ruined manor house beckoned with empty window frames. Was it here, amidst bawling calves and cackling, free-roaming hens, that the chancellor had pledged himself to the reconciliation of Germans and Poles? I don't understand. Then the sexton points to an equally dilapidated little house behind the ruined manor and says, "Kreisau Circle." Of course! Count von Moltke, Yorck von Wartenburg, Delp, Reichwein. Of course! This was where the Kreisau Circle organized its resistance against Hitler—most of them were executed after the failed assassination attempt on July 20, 1944—and so the chancellor of the Federal Republic had come here to show his respect for the German antifascist resistance, which the Poles honor as well.

A noble gesture. As it turned out, the chancellor's Polish hosts had forced it on him at the last minute. He was initially slated to appear in Góra Świętej Anny, formerly Annaberg, a town in Upper Silesia where the bulk of the German-speaking minority resides. Annaberg, too, is a place of symbolic importance: the Nazis erected a memorial there, complete with an outdoor theater, for those Germans who died fighting the Poles during the plebiscite-related uprisings of 1920–21. The Poles blew up the Nazi memorial in 1945 and replaced it with a monument honoring the Poles. Going there to celebrate a reconciliation between Poles and Germans displayed the same delicacy of feeling that Helmut Kohl had last shown at Bitburg. And when his hosts expressed fears of demonstrations for a Greater Germany, the chancellor sprang blithely to the other extreme, into the footsteps of the resistance fighter Helmut von Moltke from Krzyżowa.

Apparently the event was total chaos. A mass was read in Polish in the tiny church on the von Moltke estate. The Germans countered by singing their own hymn to Saint Anne, but no one heard them because the Poles controlled the microphone and filled the chapel with their songs.

And what about the banner with the slogan HELMUT, YOU'RE OUR CHANCELLOR TOO? The sexton didn't speak a word of German, and she didn't understand the slogan. "You'll just have to go to Swidnice or Wrocław for that— there aren't any Germans around here."

Wrocław's Hotel Monopol, constructed in 1871 with French reparation payments following the Franco-Prussian War, exudes the musty pomp of that era. No sooner do we drive up than several helpful souls come running out. To my surprise, the dignified old gentleman in livery who reaches for my leather bag speaks flawless Italian. He proudly informs me that he fought against the Germans in Italy with Władysław Anders's army. I don't like seeing the old man carry my bag, but there's no point in arguing. On the way to our room, the metal tag with our room number keeps falling off the key ring, which simply won't stay closed. The old man continues to smile apologetically as he bends over with dignity and slips the tag back onto the ring, only to repeat the motion over and over until it becomes the very image of futility.

Jan Mondry, who comes to breakfast the following morning, is a lay reader for the German Protestant congregation in Wrocław (Breslau) and an active member of the German Union there. Right from the start, he puts us at ease with his wit and worldliness: Mondry is no Germanizer, and he seems perfectly happy in his Polish surroundings; he can barely cope with all the requests for German lessons. As a former railroadman, he's been around, and proves also to be a strongly rooted person with an incredible memory. He knows five decades of the timetable on the Breslau–Berlin run, as well as the complicated construction history of the city's landmark buildings. Adjusting borders, revanchist schemes—he has no interest in such things, and he only laughs in his clear tenor voice at Herbert Czaja's Deportee League. What he wants sounds more sensible than alarming: to speak German, to read German masses, and, last but not least, to sing—yes, sing—Schumann lieder! What about the banner HELMUT, YOU'RE OUR CHANCELLOR TOO? Mondry gives an amused laugh: "It must have been the crowd from Upper Silesia. But I doubt they wanted to cause any trouble." He's ready with a benign interpretation: the Upper Silesians just wanted to remind the chancellor of his promise to aid the German minority.

In Upper Silesia, Mondry tells us, the Polish Communist regime took an impossible stand: for over forty years it tried to resolve the issue of the German minority by steadfastly denying that it existed.

This is confirmed by Ryszard Borski, the Polish pastor who ministers to the Protestant congregation in Wrocław and Jawor (Jauer). The little town of Jawor contains one of the finest Protestant churches of the pre-Baroque period in Central Europe, Kościół Pokoju, the Church of Peace of the Holy Ghost. The half-timbered structure was opened to the public only a few years ago; twenty of the faithful now gather every Sunday in a space that could accommodate six hundred. "After the war," the pastor tells us, "the Communist regime wanted people to forget that Silesia had been under German cultural domination for over six hundred years." He himself was surprised when he took up his office in Silesia to discover how German everything was: "Most of the old buildings, the town halls, the churches, all show their German past." The official line, borrowed from Stalin, was that "historic justice" had returned to the Poles their ancestral realms—and this propaganda has proved effective. The pastor offers an example. He once ordered some beams to repair the timbering on the church. The truck driver who delivered them was struck by the wood paintings that covered every inch of the interior walls of the church, and asked how they got there. The pastor couldn't make him understand that the church had been built by the Hapsburgs, not by the Poles. Now, how could that be, this was Poland, wasn't it! When the pastor explained to him that practically no Poles had lived there between 1335 and 1945, the truck driver broke off the conversation in fury; he considered the information unpatriotic.

The pastor vehemently defended the rights of the Upper Silesian minority: "Why shouldn't they fight for recognition?" He believed the candidacy of the German Henryk Krol in the 1989 municipal elections in Opole (formerly Oppeln) was a healthy surprise to most Poles. At least it reminded them that there were still Germans in Poland. And what about that banner in Krzyżowa?

Pastor Borski rules out the possibility of Germans in his congregation wanting to challenge the borders. What's more, he doesn't know of any Polish group that would want to revise the eastern borders either. And in Upper Silesia? Are revanchist elements still active there? At this, the pastor shakes his head and prefers not to commit himself. "In a new Europe," he says cautiously, letting his gaze rise to meet the distant future, "we will have to do away with the existing borders through economic and cultural exchange, and not draw new ones."

Well said, Father, but who the devil waved that banner? Our trip has turned into a wild-goose chase. In my quest for the culprit, I make a last stop at Opole. We visit Henryk Krol's house, a "paired house," as the Polonized version of the German "semi-detached" is called. A Polish woman in her thirties answers the door—Henryk Krol's wife. She knows almost no German, she and her husband obviously speak Polish at home. Well, so far it seems Henryk Krol doesn't eat Poles for breakfast.

Since he won't be back until evening, I talk with his father, Johann.

Krol senior has a Biblical way with language and describes his lifelong efforts this way: "We wanted to call the spirits of this place back into the light of day. Glemp, Rakowski, Jaruzelski, and the rest of their high priests had banished us to the shadows. We didn't exist." The existence of the German minority was denied right up to 1990, "while all along this region had belonged to Germany until 1920, and it's nonsense to say there weren't any Germans in Germany, now come on!" Krol senior doesn't mention the fact that Silesian ties to "Germany" haven't always been so smooth. In the struggle for power among the Austrians, the Prussians, and ultimately the Poles, the Silesians got pushed back and forth, but no one ever really asked where they might like to belong; so they learned to consider themselves first and foremost Silesians. Among themselves, they speak a Slavic-German creole—*gwara śląska*—that reveals their cross-cultural identity. After the war, the Silesians were forcibly Polonized: "We were frightened, we shat in our pants, we're still frightened." Krol senior angrily tells us about a neighbor, "a pure-blooded German," who still refuses to admit he's German. It was only thanks to Gorbachev that the minority issue came up at all. Krol doesn't conceal the fact that the Germans in Opole took a page from the Poles, that is to say the Polish minority in Lithuania. "Suddenly all sorts of minorities are speaking out, so why shouldn't we?" The German Union in Opole was finally recognized on January 31, 1990—recognized but still not registered. "Of course now that the Poles see us, you Germans don't see us anymore."

In the push for unification, he maintains, the Germans in Poland were totally forgotten. "No one gave us anything, not even a photocopier." The Kohl visit was a fraud from beginning to end. He hadn't done anything for the minority. "And the thing is, we wouldn't cost anyone much. We like it here!" The only dependable ally the Germans had was Solidarity. He couldn't believe how cooperative they had been; when someone shredded and defaced his son Henryk Krol's campaign posters, Solidarity had publicly defended the German candidate and condemned the vandalism. Krol senior rejects the claims that the Deportee League spokespersons are making on Silesia. "What do Czaja's people think they're doing?" he asks. "We live less than 100 miles from the border. Are we supposed to kick out the Poles who settled here after 1945? That would be just as unfair as what happened to us. And who would come here after that— the deportees? They've got it too good in West Germany."

And what about the banner in Krzyżowa? "I don't know who made it," Johann Krol says. But someone had to, right? Maybe even the League of Deportees in West Germany? He laughs. I can still hear him saying: "This is our home here, so we're harmless. But the deportees, now there you're going to find some troublemakers."

I take my leave of the old man, thinking about Indian chieftains on the reservation, and with a surprisingly simple conclusion: The Germans now in Silesia are not fierce revanchists but modest people pursuing modest goals in modest two-family dwellings. They want no more than what any minority has a right to: their language, their history, their costume, and their singing groups— so what if I don't like their songs? Most of all, though, they want an end to discrimination. Who in the world needs to fear these old people, desperately trying to keep their own children in line? Because they know that, sooner or later, their zither playing won't be any match for Michael Jackson and Tina Turner. And besides, they've long since mixed with the Poles, both in their language and in their genes. There they sit, typing out their pamphlets with two fingers in a Polonized German, without fax machines or photocopiers, trying to find a place for themselves in a homeland that has changed irrevocably.

Still looking for my culprit, I return to my starting point, Berlin. At Germany House, headquarters for the various refugee organizations, I sit facing the chairman of the Silesian Patriots' Clubs, Kraffto von Metnitz. I feel duped, because even he turns out to be a paper tiger. Sure, he sticks to the right-wing position that the Oder-Neisse line can't be recognized until the Allies and Germany sign the peace treaty that has been deferred since 1945. But when I ask him what he thinks will follow once an accord is signed, he says: recognition. And what if things don't work out that way? Would he go back to Silesia, I ask, if Czaja's fantasies came true?

Von Metnitz answers without hesitation. He has gotten used to living among Germans, he says, and at his age has no desire to learn a foreign language. And like a lot of Silesians, he's distressed by what's happened to his former home. His last visit, a few years back, was "an eye-opener."

He had traveled to Krobielowice (formerly Krieblowitz), a village that Frederick William III, king of Prussia, had bestowed on Field Marshal von Blücher. Von Metnitz knew the Polish teacher there and accompanied him to General Blücher's mausoleum. Where is Blücher's coffin? von Metnitz asked. According to the teacher, the coffin had been moved into a neighbor's attic. And Blücher's bones? Taken out and buried somewhere! The neighbor was already looking forward to his handsome coffin, the Polish teacher continued—you couldn't get anything of that quality in Poland today. He was only afraid his wife might die first, because then he'd have to let her take it. "So there you see," von Metnitz concluded with a sigh, "how the Poles continue to live off what the Germans have done!"

I neglected to ask von Metnitz about the banner in Krzyżowa. But if I can't put a name to the culprit, at least I think I know where he stands politically: his tracks lead not to the German minority in Poland, but west to the Deportee League and the *Republikaner* Party. The agitators who still lay German claim to regions lost in the East have settled far west of the Oder-Neisse line. With his endless equivocations on the subject of the border, Chancellor Kohl made clear how much these firebrands still influence West German politics.

His temporizing was a foreign relations disaster, and

it can hardly have made life any easier for the German minority in Poland. It did accomplish his goal on the domestic political scene, though: Kohl showed the Deportee League diehards that they could still get their chancellor's ear. His performance was an unscrupulous display of smoke and mirrors, totally lacking in historical shame but extremely successful, because it allowed him to freeze out the extreme right-wing *Republikaner* who had appropriated the "eastern lands" issue and were taking a dangerously large number of votes away from his Christian Democrats. Kohl managed to reduce them below the all-important 5-percent level in the local elections of spring 1990 and in the first all-German elections in December as well. (In the old Federal Republic as in the larger new one, a party has to have at least 5 percent of the vote to have a seat in the Bundestag.) Having done so, the chancellor then revealed—just in time for the "two-plus-four" talks in July 1990—that he was committed to reconciliation with the Poles. So he ultimately added an international coup to his domestic one: the whole world was relieved when he finally accepted the western border of Poland, as though he had had to wrench it out of himself after intolerable pain and soul-searching. Friend and foe applauded a concession that had previously been regarded as a *sine qua non* of German unity. Kohl's high-wire act had turned a dead issue back into a bargaining chip.

Connoisseurs of political power plays may admire Kohl's bluffing. But his success will be short-lived; it will make him a hostage to forces he has outfoxed but not defeated. It is clear that revanchist sentiment in the

Federal Republic will gain support from East Germany. East German teenagers have already crossed the bridge into Poland at Zgorzelec (formerly Görlitz) and defaced walls with pan-German graffiti. *The New York Times* (December 3, 1990) reported that, on the eve of the day the two Germanys were reunited, several hundred teenagers armed with knives and Molotov cocktails went on a rampage in the East German border towns of Guben and Cottbus, protesting the surrender of German territories to Poland. Their banners and most likely the rest of their paraphernalia came from the leaders of the League, who never tire of condemning the "surrender of one quarter of the German state."

Of course, even the deportees understand they cannot undo the official recognition of Poland's western border—but they're determined to go down fighting. The Christian Democrats won't keep them in check by speeches alone. In 1990, they received five times as much money out of the Kohl government for "preserving the cultural heritage of Germany" as they did in 1983— 20.4 million D-marks. The sum is earmarked for the German minority in Poland. Since the League controls the funds, however, a new—and not merely financial— dependency is in store for the Silesians: in fact, the League has demanded that the Federal government not interfere in any of its "collaborative relations." The results of this collaboration are already evident: the bilingual *Upper Silesian News* can't compete with the new and exclusively German-language tabloid *Silesia News*, which is rapidly forcing it out of business.

Still, I'm willing to bet such tirades from the dim past are the League's last gasp before it sinks into oblivion. As the Germans in Poland begin to secure and exercise their rights as a minority, the League agitators will lose their credibility. Their ideologically rigid leadership relies on a petrified notion called "communism," and will never survive a true democratization of Eastern and Central Europe—if such a democratization actually occurs, and if it ultimately leads the way out of an economic collapse.

If these "ifs" don't happen, though, the most outlandish scenarios remain possible. There's a rumor that not only German-speaking extremists but even some Poles wouldn't mind if Silesia "came home to the Reich." Not because they've suddenly discovered an affection for the Germans, but because annexation offers deutsche marks and the quickest way out of economic misery.

• • • • •

Some People Can Even Sleep Through an Earthquake

They finally found it in January 1990, the much-sought phrase needed to cushion our slide into the post-Communist era. Egon Krenz, former secretary general of the Socialist Unity Party, had the privilege of introducing it—almost in passing—into the language of the day. When questioned about his role in the Leipzig election fraud of the previous spring,* he stated for the record: "From the present perspective, it seems to me that our elections in East Germany were never really free and secret."

Not one of the ever-dour participants at that meeting laughed or applauded Krenz's new application of the Heisenberg uncertainty principle. In lay scientific terms, the secretary's statement could be rephrased like this:

---

* Krenz, as the election officer, apparently saw to it that 10 to 15 percent of the uncast ballots (which had been withheld to boycott the election) were counted for the Socialist Unity Party. Despite this election rigging, the Party made its poorest showing in forty years, receiving 98.4 percent of the vote. In the excitement over the rigging, people almost forgot that an "honest" count would still have given the Socialist Unity Party a comfortable absolute majority of about 83 percent.

The appearance of a given subject—say, electoral fraud—
depends completely on the observer's perspective. Not
being, but time (or, in fact, the exact date) determines
consciousness!

But it wouldn't have mattered if they had laughed,
because the motto "From the present perspective" describes, with unprecedented conciseness, the intellectual balancing act that became a popular sport after
November 9. Players must combine traditional school
figures with new, diametrically opposed movements, all
without falling off the bar. The goal of the exercise is a
speedy and skilled descent—in sports language, this is
called "landing on your feet."

The extreme versatility of Krenz's phrase demonstrates its worth. It brings to mind countless examples
and variants the minute you hear it. All the spectacular
dislocations, painful splits, and even withdrawals due to
injury noticed in the media skirmishes suddenly make
sense. Take language: speech and writing have changed
almost overnight. Whole areas of everyday political jar-
gon have been abandoned, while others, long forgotten,
are suddenly being rediscovered and resettled. You
hardly ever hear the word "Communist" anymore, except in connection with the word "catastrophe." The
concept "socialism" is only used with the hasty adjectival
prefix "democratic," or else not at all. Mystifying variants
include "socialist socialism" or "socialist free enterprise."
And what happened, by the way, to that previously common notion, the "anti-Communist"? That hoary insult
seems on its way to becoming an honorific.

Because, from the present perspective, it turns out

that almost no one in East Germany was ever an ardent, or even just an active, Communist. The whole country seems to have been a kind of halfway house for ideologically abused adults. And, from the present perspective, the Socialist Unity Party and its partners in the ruling coalition were, like the NSDAP before them, a headquarters for covert resistance fighters—so covert, in fact, that people hardly noticed them, all the way up to the end, even though they had managed to infiltrate the highest levels. If one is to believe Erich Honecker's testimony before the East German public prosecutor, the Socialist Unity Party's top man spent his last years in office fighting his own government.

East Germans are by no means the only ones performing this exercise: passionate practitioners may be found on both sides of the border. Anyone with a memory (or an archive) will be amazed at how quickly and adroitly people can exchange old positions and convictions for more current ones. "Stabilize East Germany," "Dump Reunification"—such causes had vocal advocates not so long ago, and often for good reason. The affection Helmut Kohl has recently shown for words like "demonstration" and "revolution" is amazing. And it's strange to see rather senior standard-bearers among the conservatives— Joachim Fest, Karl Heinz Bohrer, Johannes Gross, consistent and often brilliant defenders of the elite—suddenly catching up to 1968 and discovering their love for the people.

I'd like to make something clear from the start: I consider the right to change your mind, to make mistakes and recant them, a fundamental human right. It should be expected, and even hoped, that major events affect and change the way people think. The recognition of past mistakes and the ability to question are some of the most valuable gifts thinking people can bestow on their contemporaries. Much of the scientific method is built on the identification of errors: there is almost no advance in scientific knowledge that does not depend on naming and then discarding false or inadequate hypotheses. So I am far from criticizing a change of mind or conviction: my remarks are aimed at the silent maneuvering, the blurring of contradictions between past and present positions, the calculated, covert slide into the present tense. In a talk he gave in 1981, Karl Popper formulated a criterion necessary for every genuine process of learning: "The new, fundamental law is that in order to avoid mistakes as much as possible, we must learn from the ones we do commit. Thus the concealment of mistakes is the greatest intellectual sin."

Let us expand Popper's notion of "mistake." We learn not only from our mistakes, but also from the correction of insights that were once accurate but now suddenly prove inadequate. The policy of "gradualism" was by no means a mistake, but an advance that eventually reached an "end." "End" is how Willy Brandt described the watershed of 1989. He is also one of the few politicians who didn't hesitate, even long ago, to call certain ways of thinking (like the decree against radicals) by their proper name.

If every advance in knowledge involves the exercise of memory, then in Germany our ability to learn is imperiled. Because German self-righteousness presents an insuperable obstacle to levelheaded reflection. People who openly admit that they have to rethink something or that they made a mistake are seen as intellectual cowards. Almost any turn of phrase that describes this process is either negative or strikingly theatrical in tone. We "confess a mistake," we "abandon our position," we "shift our stand." Even the relatively harmless "change of heart" sounds disreputable in political discourse. The archaic ideal of Nibelung loyalty still counts more than the desire for knowledge. Which is why major conceptual upheavals always tend to elicit two apparently very different reactions in Germany: stubborn persistence or energetic reversal. The latter is of course blood brother to the former—since every change of conviction is tainted with betrayal and consequently accompanied by heavy feelings of guilt. This is why these reversals happen so quickly, as people make their flying leaps onto the bandwagon.

Even before the Wall fell, I had begun to wonder how some of my friends and acquaintances were dealing with the chaos of events. After all, opportunities for confusion existed long before the summer of 1989. I myself was no exception. For example, I still remember quite clearly the unpleasant dizziness I felt when, shortly after Gorbachev came to power, the Kremlin acknowledged that the positioning of its medium-range SS-20 and SS-22 missiles was a unilateral build-up and should be considered part of an offensive military strategy. Had I heard right? Was the highest representative of that peace-loving power echoing Helmut Schmidt, while I and many of my embattled comrades at the Berlin Writers' Peace Forum had claimed the Soviet missiles were purely defensive? Now what? Either Gorbachev was a fool, or I was. This earth-shaking political question was subsequently resolved at the Geneva Disarmament Talks: the missiles positioned earlier by the Russians were to be totally withdrawn by May 1991, in exchange for the withdrawal of the more recently positioned American missiles. But did anyone take advantage of this great opportunity to reflect publicly on an error of judgment? Did I?

I have similar questions for some of the spokespersons from liberal, leftist, and "alternative" political groups. Pretty much everyone was happy about the opening of the Wall. People gave credit where credit was due: much, of course, to Gorbachev, but also to the citizens' rights movements in East Germany and the other Eastern bloc nations. But this hearty agreement with the East German opposition and dissidents is of fairly recent vintage, and didn't become the majority position for a long time. The Greens—usually mavericks like Petra Kelly, Otto Schily, Joschka Fischer, Gerd Bastian, and Jutta Ditfurth—declared their solidarity early on. It was, notably, a Green delegation that, on its first visit to Moscow, honored the victims of fascism and then called for a memorial to the victims of Stalinism. But such gestures remained the exception. At a Peace Movement conference in Frankfurt in February 1984, for example, a 60–40 majority refused to declare its solidarity with the arrested members of the Weimar-based "Monday Circle," pioneers of the 1989 revolution. People didn't want to provoke "East Germany, the peace power" that had declared all independent peace initiatives illegal. Are these "friends of peace" celebrating now, and in what way? Is there nothing here that needs to be explained, nothing to set right, nothing to remember? And where are all the loyalists who until not so long ago went straight for the jugular when you called East Germany a Stalinist dictatorship?

I'm not asking for confessions, lamentations, a literature of suffering and martyrdom. But a word of reflection, maybe even an occasional apology—just a little effort at remembering would prove that people really are looking for insights, not places to hide.

West German leftists spared themselves the shock that French intellectuals felt on reading Solzhenitsyn's *Gulag Archipelago*; instead, they put their energies into an angry critique of French shortsightedness. They themselves, however, never really abandoned the discretion they had long practiced in describing Stalin's camps as a "mistake." When the word "crime" was finally uttered, they avoided the debate and sought refuge in equivocations: "Yes, but on the other hand . . ." They referred to "the by no means insignificant crimes of Stalinism," or "the model Cuban revolution, despite its persecution of homosexuals," or "the by no means easy fate of dissidents." They managed to dodge every challenge to their worldview by pointing out that the Soviet Union was under siege, and by quoting Brecht: "The escape from capitalist barbarism may entail some barbarism of its own."

The Social Democratic Party did no better. While it was momentarily uplifting to hear party leaders at the special convention in Berlin (December 18–20, 1989) speak of "fulfilling an ancient Social Democratic dream," their interpretation of this dream was somewhat bewildering since they read it to mean the sudden prospect of German unity. Yet, the party platform articulated earlier in 1989 and designed for the next thirty years made no mention of this "ancient dream." It simply stated: "The national issue remains subordinate to the demands of peace." But what would happen in the event that unrest in East Germany actually threatened the status quo? On September 22, 1989, Helmut Schmidt—presumably still representing a consensus of the Social Democratic Party—addressed this question: "An upheaval in East Germany would endanger the reform process in all of Eastern Europe. The German Question will not be resolved until the next century."

The implicit message to East German citizens was: Keep still. They did not heed his advice—as no one then foresaw but everyone now knows. They risked an upheaval, which not only did not endanger the reform process for one immediate neighbor, Czechoslovakia, but actually fostered it. Against all expectation, such things do sometimes happen in history. Why can't people admit it? Why pretend continuity where none exists?

So far, I've only considered halfhearted forays into what one might call the periphery of the political earthquake of 1989. A thorough tour of this zone shows how the left has, in recent years, repeatedly downplayed popular demands for freedom in countries on the other side of the Wall by citing a fear of conflict it all too quickly ennobles as "concern for world peace." At the epicenter of the earthquake of 1989 stands a system called socialism.

No one can claim that the German left has now confronted this challenge. Its intellectual response falls primarily under the heading of damage control. The left's main goal is to preserve as much ideological comfort as possible. In good Darwinian fashion, the breakup of former ideological holdings is left to historical selection: certain opinions and ideas have clearly proven they are not historically "viable." But no one really wants to know which those are, and whether they will be replaced, or what might replace them. "It looks like socialism will have to go underground for the next thirty years!" This purely tactical reaction is what passes for analysis. Such half-baked thought serves to calm, to pacify, to reassure—but not to understand. Some people can even sleep through an earthquake.

And not just a tremor, but an earthquake that tops the Richter scale. The watershed year of 1989 can be compared only with 1945, which it surpasses in intellectual significance. Back then, a pseudophilosophy marked from its inception by misanthropy and racism was finally forced to capitulate. The historical turning point of 1989 has a different character. The political embodiment of a utopia that had inspired the best and the brightest of many generations finally gave up the ghost. The great social experiment that had run for seventy years, and more or less forcibly involved over 250 million people, had to be broken off because it was constantly breaking down. This is an event of epochal dimensions, every bit as significant as the cataclysms that ended the Christian Middle Ages following the discoveries by Giordano Bruno and Galileo Galilei. And this failure cannot be explained by arguing that the theory was simply misapplied. In accordance with the wishes of its founders and organizers, socialism was devised as a "scientific" doctrine. And if an experiment continues to fail for seventy years, the source of error must be sought in its original hypothesis as well as in its execution.

Heroic persistence is rarer and more appealing than energetic reversal, but appeal is no substitute for persuasion. With all due respect for her obstinacy, the Greens' spokesperson, Jutta Ditfurth, should be held accountable for a statement she made on January 26, 1990, during a panel discussion at Humboldt University. She said she didn't feel the need to respond when someone demanded she revise her model of socialism, because those countries where socialist theory had been put into practice, and which were now declaring themselves bankrupt in every way, had never been truly socialist to begin with. So socialism hadn't failed. The only thing that had failed was capitalism, because it had proven itself incapable of stopping the destruction of the environment. Great. Now that we've managed to save our worldview, let's move on.

I've already admitted the validity of such an argument: the failure of an experiment doesn't necessarily disprove its premises. You don't have to doubt Mozart because Igor Oistrakh plays him badly. But when every virtuoso makes the same piece sound bad, you have every right to suspect the composer. The flat assertion that present-day socialism in no way detracts from the theory ultimately amounts to intellectual shirking. It may be reassuring, but it only avoids the problem of deciding which components of the theory will sink with the wreck of socialism and which might still be salvaged.

A brief question to Jutta Ditfurth and her colleagues: How do you do it? These days we all spend a lot of time reading the paper and watching TV. What do you think, for example, when you hear our foreign minister, Hans Dietrich Genscher, talking about "forty years of socialist mismanagement"? For a second, the old reflexes come into play: "Cold warrior, anti-Communist hack." But in the light of the daily news, these reflexes have to yield to an admission that Genscher is simply stating the facts. Or when you see the chairman of the Bundesbank, Karl Otto Pöhl, explaining the advantages of capitalism to workers in a state-run factory as confidently and unabashedly as ever? Fortunately, he faces some opposition: the workers ask anxious questions about the less glamorous consequences of a free enterprise economy—unemployment, pensions, the status of women, daycare, etc. The West German speakers are well prepared, they have the figures at their fingertips. Comparisons show that in just about every area, even the environment, capitalist West Germany comes off better. The workers nod, fall silent, hope. West Germany has never looked so good as it does in comparison with East Germany. So if you really want to criticize the way we do business, you'll have to go pretty far beyond East Germany to find a point of departure. The only question is where—Nicaragua, Cuba, China?

All right, so none of this upsets your "model of socialism." But the revelations don't stop there: Over five million State Security Police files! Plans uncovered for gigantic internment camps containing "negative-hostile elements"! The exploitation of 60,000 Vietnamese slave workers! A world record for environmental pollution! Just between us, if we had read all of this in some Western tabloid a year ago, we would have dismissed it as slanderous provocation. To tell the truth: even what we might have known, we didn't want to believe.

All right, all right, those were Stalinist distortions of socialism—"No socialism without freedom!" But, by the way, wasn't it Lenin who did away with democracy? That's what Rosa Luxemburg said so long ago; at least we've still got her. But what if the catastrophic economic failure of socialism today were due not only to a lack of democracy but also to the suppression of private ownership? That would certainly challenge a central piece of the doctrine. Doesn't it look as though events have proven our worst enemies correct? Doesn't it seem these days that history itself has judged the duel between socialism and capitalism, and declared capitalism the winner? And isn't this winner now commanding from the mount: Thou shalt have no other social system besides me!?

My congratulations to anyone whose faith has not been shaken. But I'm afraid that those who don't feel doubts also won't be able to resist them in the long run. And those who do resist with eyes blindfolded and ears covered may well be saints, but they are not prophets.

A stubborn hope has it that "independent" writers and thinkers are more unsparing in their pursuit of the truth than others, because they must answer only to themselves. Earlier than most, and often at great personal risk, a few such "independent" writers from East Germany exposed the Stalinist ossification of socialism. In their writings, they prepared the ground for the citizens' movements. Only under the magnifying glass of the October Revolution of 1989 did it become fully clear these literary "dissidents" had almost always remained committed to one assumption in their critique: they never questioned the legitimacy of the socialist one-party state. Nor the party's right to rule. They criticized the Socialist Unity Party's abuse of power, not its monopoly of it; their demands for more democracy were meant not to secure free elections and a ("bourgeois-reactionary") multiparty system, but to eliminate censorship and build a plurality of opinion within the socialist power structure. Interestingly, East German literature doesn't know the figure of the "valiant refugee." Whoever denied the state his loyalty and left it of his own accord was considered a traitor: anyone who did not criticize from the socialist perspective could not hope for solidarity.

Now that a peaceful revolution has burst the bounds of this critique, the erstwhile groundbreakers find themselves facing an intellectual dilemma. They can—and some do—stick to their old reformist positions and consequently declare the revolution a wrong turn. Such a stance is consistent and deserves respect. But those critical-but-loyal writers who welcomed the October Revolution of 1989 can do so credibly only if they subject their earlier positions to critical review. Writers, however, suffer from a professional disability called vanity: What do you ignoramuses think you're doing, calling us to task? I was already saying that back in 19__. You mean you haven't read that piece?

Heroes prefer self-quotation to self-doubt. Their self-righteousness displaces productive curiosity about how and why they once thought differently, maybe even incorrectly. It's quite something to see the old men of "a better socialism" making their peace on one talk show after another with what is, after all, the antisocialist revolution of 1989. They outdo each other quoting articles to prove who predicted what when and before whom. There's only one thing missing, one thing they won't say: Maybe I made a mistake on this one point, I'll have to think about it, I don't really know, I can't comment right now. Just like politicians, the chiefs of dissent march beneath the banner: "Whatever you do, just be sure to save face."

The Communist writer and poet Stephan Hermlin gave a good demonstration of self-righteousness in a March 1990 interview for the periodical *Neue Deutsche Literatur*. He's an aggressive antifascist, and I wouldn't reproach him here for certain oversights if he hadn't repeatedly criticized others for this same flaw. "Some people," according to Hermlin, "suffer from lapses of memory. They no longer remember exactly where they stood five or ten years ago and put on airs, proclaim themselves great reformers. Only they aren't—they're fellow travelers of reform."

As in earlier interviews, Stephan Hermlin shows he is a committed proponent of Gorbachev's *glasnost* and *perestroika*. As such, no one has forced him to take a position on his three now ancient paeans to Stalin.* But when he chooses to do so himself, the results are amazingly self-indulgent. Like everyone else, he has experienced "conversions," and besides, his praise of the tyrant puts him in good company—Aragon, Eluard, Picasso, Rivera, Brecht, Becher, Mayakovsky, and others. This accurate observation might be the starting point for an excursus on the fallibility of intellectuals—Hermlin's Polish contemporary Czesław Milosz launched that theme some forty years ago in his book *The Captive Mind*. The fact that a lot of famous men made a mistake at the same time doesn't make it less egregious. But Hermlin says nothing to that effect. Instead of expressing self-doubt in a form that only idiots would try to use against him, he contents himself with the statement, "I have no reason to be ashamed of these things," and invites us to reflect on "interesting philosophic-aesthetic questions." There are "murderous figures who—rightly or wrongly—embody a specific value or a vision, which is why art wants access to them." Now, it makes a difference whether art is looking to criticize or worship

---

* A typical sample:
>   From the eternal converse of islands and nations,
>   Delight arises with tidings in hand,
>   Where promises live and eras are changing,
>   Our time at last pronounces its name: Stalin.

these "murderous figures." Other great names have vouched for this distinction, but does Hermlin mention them? Not a one! He proudly sets himself apart from "certain renegades" who "have changed their positions countless times in the course of their lives. . . . That is foreign to me." A questionable assertion—fortunately for him, I might add. Because so far as I know, he never applied the adjective "murderous" to Stalin before. In a 1984 TV interview, he made the following comment about his Stalin poems: "How could I recant them, when millions of people died with the words 'bread, Stalin, fatherland!' on their lips?" At the time, Gorbachev wasn't yet in office. But even then, and decades earlier, some of Hermlin's colleagues had publicly asked the opposite question: "How many people died with the curse 'Stalin, that murderer!' on their lips?"

Why can't a writer of Stephan Hermlin's stature finally show some respect for these fellow writers? Why can't he say, along with Christa Wolf: "We need to explore our own 'difficulties with the truth,' and we will find that we, too, have reason to feel regret and shame"?

It is true that Hermlin repeatedly helped fellow East German writers who were being harassed and forced to leave the country, even when, as was often the case, he had a low opinion of their literary efforts. His unflinching support for the East Germany of Erich Honecker, whom he had known since his youth, earned him many enemies in the West, and he took the resulting damage in stride. He defended the socialist utopianism of his youth, born of the struggle against fascism, against all the objections raised by reality. And yet, in order to maintain his hope (and his assertion) that the first socialist state on German soil did not depend on censorship, he frequently had to rely on personal intervention. Thanks to his phone calls, censorship of individual writers was often lifted, and exit permits granted. The fact that he, a writer, thus found himself acting indirectly as a functionary of the state must have bothered him, but it didn't fundamentally affect his loyalty.

In the interview I mentioned before, Hermlin cites his services as a defender of free speech. As far back as thirty years ago, he notes, he and Anna Seghers protested the exclusion of Heiner Müller. Referring to the deportation of Wolf Biermann (1976) and the exclusion first of "twelve" and, later, another "eight or nine" writers, he protests the "extraordinary amnesia" of people who forget "the simple fact that in 1979 two people made long speeches challenging the Writers Union to vote against the exclusions. One of those two was me."

The interview ends on that note of self-congratulation. But since we're talking about amnesia, it's worth mentioning something else Hermlin said about those who, after the inexcusable campaign against Wolf Biermann and others, left East Germany and began meeting in West Berlin at what became known as the "Refugee Forum." "These gentlemen are simply emigrants," he said, "people who emigrated lock, stock, and barrel by light of day, with their papers in order, of their own free will and often on friendly terms." This statement was pure insult. Some of those "emigrant" colleagues had spent time in prison, others had been blackmailed into leaving East Germany by being told they would never publish there—almost none left of their own free will. Why can't Hermlin admit that he let his utopia blind him? That kind of confession would do more to ease the "spiritual and moral distress of our society" (Christa Wolf's words) than the assertion, easily refuted, that he was always on the right track.

To cite Karl Popper again: "We intellectuals have done terrible things, we pose a great threat. Not only are we arrogant, but we can be bought."

This statement is interesting for its use both of the first-person plural and the word "threat." We intellectuals, trained to be defiant, tend to feel flattered when someone classifies us as a "threat." That is why we ought to identify the "threat." The great crimes against society in this century were committed in the name of some "idea." We intellectuals discovered the idea, though usually not its execution, and we writers supported it and sang its praises. And all too often we sang the praises not only of the idea, but also of its execution.

Writers and intellectuals have recently taken to claiming they should be counted among the endangered species. That may be. But for the sake of accuracy, one should add that they are also among the most dangerous species.

Those who hoped East German writers would take advantage of the opportunity for a vigorous debate on these matters—now that, at last, they had no one to answer to but themselves—attended the Extraordinary Session of the Writers Union in Berlin in March 1990. A general meeting of the local power plant, even a dentists' convention, would have been a more joyous occasion, especially in the wake of a successful popular revolution. Instead of euphoria, the congress was marked by a sadness so oppressive it seemed as if a mass suicide were being planned. No one celebrated the defeat of dictatorship or the end of censorship, but neither did anyone express guilt or sorrow at the collapse of a worldview that had until quite recently stood intact.

Christa Wolf's question, whether all those now posing as victims of censorship had really suffered from it, met with applause and nothing more. An investigation of the Union's Stalinist past was referred to committee right at the start: "We have to look to the future." This move was justified by the chairman, Hermann Kant, who, though not present because of "a heart problem," sent a greeting to the congress in which he claimed the Union represented that part of East Germany that had always supported "a plurality of views," as well as various other democratic virtues. He thereby rechristened as a resistance organization a union that had earlier pledged itself "to the role of leading the working class and its party." His message, in short: We have nothing to be ashamed of! The assembled writers gratefully applauded; not one person booed.

Opening this truly "extraordinary" session, the writer Volker Braun expressly stated his "respect" for his absent predecessor who had "held office during trying times," but rejected demands that he accede to his post. Neither Christa Wolf nor Christoph Hein had any desire to, either. The poet Rainer Kirsch finally accepted, and in his speech approvingly quoted Volker Braun, who had approvingly quoted Hermann Kant, and then made himself popular by once again warning against accusatory investigations of the Union's history.

To usher in the new democratic era, the Writers Union elected to defend the privileges it had received under the dictatorship. The East German Writers Union was the wealthiest of its kind in Europe. It received 93.5 percent of its funding from the government and other public sources. The complaint that writers' "artistic and social existence" would be threatened in a society where "art is a commodity and market forces decide" conceals the real drama here. Hitherto sustained by and loyal to the state, East German art is now trading this dependency on the state for a dependency on the market. You could argue over which dependency is better, but at this stage it's really six of one, half a dozen of the other.

The writers shunned every question of any interest: Why didn't the East German opposition produce a dissident like Václav Havel, Adam Michnik, or György Konrád? Why did East German intellectuals leave the simple demands—"Down with the dictatorship of the Socialist Unity Party! Free elections in East Germany!"—to the Monday demonstrators in Leipzig? Why did East German dissent always stay within the system?

Did they talk in hushed voices because they rightly feared that any critique of East German socialism—as opposed to that of Poland, Hungary, or Czechoslovakia— would mean the complete absorption of the Democratic Republic into a united Germany? And weren't these dissidents—again unlike Poland's, Hungary's, Czechoslovakia's—hostages to a chapter in history: Never again a Greater Germany? Or was it the notoriously German lack of civic courage that accounted for the undeniable absence of energetic dissent and risk-taking? All of these difficult questions remain unaddressed in the East today.

In the West as well, where the arts and entertainment sections of leading newspapers are engaged in a hunt: the writings and speeches of East German dissidents are being parsed to determine when they last revealed traces of socialist patriotism. It is no accident that the demythification of these public figures began only once it became clear there would be no second, autonomous German state. Young arts editors, who only know about surveillance and existential distress from Kafka's *Castle*, are suddenly finding that their former favorite authors lack courage and other virtues of resistance. Character is back in vogue, and has become a measure of art. Political and aesthetic criteria have been hopelessly jumbled in this settling of scores. The question of when a writer left the Socialist Unity Party and whether he took part in this or that demonstration has suddenly acquired aesthetic importance. Anyone who stayed in the Party to the end or who still styles himself a Communist can't possibly have written any good books.

The most prominent—though by no means the only— victim of this new sport is Christa Wolf. The battle over literature and morality started with a small text that came out not long ago titled "What Remains." It tells about an experience the author had in the distant past: following the protest against the deportation of East German singer Wolf Biermann, Christa Wolf was placed under surveillance by the East German State Security Police. Drawing on notes she had compiled ten years before, she composed a short story and published it. This provoked cries of outrage from self-righteous reviewers: if she had to publish it at all, it should have come out ten years ago, not now, they said—implying that Christa Wolf was trying to give herself a political clean bill of health by publishing it. *Stern* called Christa Wolf the "national cry-baby." *Die Zeit* saw her story as a fictionalized "persecution complex" that Wolf had "managed to turn to profit as much through virtuosity as literary deceit"; and Frank Schirrmacher, the culture editor of the *Frankfurter Allgemeine Zeitung*, decided this was the right time to issue a general study documenting the writer's "authoritarian personality." Those engaged in the debate were counting on the short memory of their readers. Hadn't they just been praising the author in the same publications? Hadn't they honored her with all the prizes on the West German literary scene? The work they were now judging so sanctimoniously had been available for years. Why hadn't Frank Schirrmacher published his polemic on one of the occasions honoring Christa Wolf? A critic who asked why an author known to have supported the entry of Soviet troops into Prague should be awarded the Büchner Prize, West Germany's highest literary honor, wouldn't have been demonstrating much literary sense; but that kind of criticism would at least have indicated he had views and even some courage. Those who have taken it upon themselves to settle accounts now argue that they always had reservations but suppressed them so as not to stab East German dissidents in the back. This is nonsense: an attack in a West German paper would have only ennobled the victim in the eyes of the Party.

I don't agree with those who insist that we have no right to get involved in the internal affairs of East Germany, that we have to have been there before we can talk. We may, should, and ought to get involved everywhere. What bothers me is the self-righteousness of West Germany's literary judges. An honest appraisal would show how entangled the accusers were—and with them the whole Western half of German society—in the web of conformity and cheerleading. The accusers are carrying out their own little exercise in mastering the past, at the cost of the accused. Those who now strike postures of self-righteous reproach are only proving how much they, too, fear the past; they may be the ones who name the spirit of these times.

Civic courage is not a valid means of evaluating literature: Was Kafka the citizen a brave man? Was Goethe, Benn, or Brecht? When has a man like Schirrmacher ever shown any courage? Anyone who invokes this trait must expect to be challenged in his turn. I think Christa Wolf is a great writer; I have questions for Christa Wolf the citizen. As a citizen she may be reproached for having believed to the end that East German socialism could be reformed, despite blatant evidence to the contrary. As a writer, however, she has always been more radical, and constantly exposed herself to the wrath of the censors with her books. An important artist is now being destroyed in the West German papers, and her books are being reduced to political slogans. I hope for her sake and ours that she doesn't let herself be dragged down. Because it is she—and not her reviewers, with their easy virtue—who might use literature to sift through the ruined hopes that she shared with the best minds of her generation.

So while East German intellectuals spend their energies keeping their backs covered, and West German intellectuals spend theirs on the attack, neither camp has come to grips with the issues posed by the failure of socialism. Since the recent democratic movements began, most of the arguments and commentary from the left have resurrected the notion of the "third way," or "democratic socialism." I haven't so far been able to determine what people mean by the phrase "third way." No one up to now has described in economic terms how you can have both at once: a market economy *and* socialism, the right to work *and* market-based prices. Squaring the circle by referring to "socialist free enterprise" or "market-oriented planning" doesn't help. These turns of phrase reveal more a desire for harmony than analytic insight. The Social Democratic parties in the West haven't clarified matters much, either. Of course, they deserve much of the credit for the replacement of Manchester-style capitalism in Western Europe with mixed economies tempered with social and democratic concerns. But it's obvious that "democratic socialism" has basically remained a political rallying cry in the West, impossible to implement. Whenever Socialists or Social Democrats have come to power, they have been careful not to take the "socialization of the means of production" too seriously. True, Western Europe abounds with as many variations on capitalism as there are countries, and it's obvious that Swedish capitalism is far removed from the American version. But in all cases, we are talking about a more or less socially conscious capitalism, not about socialism.

On this subject, members of the independent intelligentsia now say they're out of their depth, and anyway, they don't know anything about economics. They're probably right, but their confession is all the more striking, since anyone who calls himself a socialist has committed himself to what is essentially an economic doctrine.

Those who don't want to argue out of pure ignorance will have to come to terms with the following four propositions—for better or for worse:

1. We probably cannot ascribe the failure of this massive seventy-year experiment in socialism exclusively to Stalinism and the lack of democracy. What has happened appears to refute the utopian notion that masses of people in the industrial age can work creatively over long periods of time for a loftier purpose than self-interest.

2. Even after 300,000 years, it's still difficult to generalize about human nature. Evidently we must reject the idea that socially undesirable tendencies like egoism, greed for private property, exploitation, aggression, racial hatred, and nationalism can be attributed to the relations of production under capitalism and can therefore be eliminated by changing those relations. Such

"flaws" are clearly as human as the sense of justice, the notion of solidarity, and the willingness to help others—though both "good" and "bad" qualities may be weakened or strengthened through socialization. Only a dictatorship could "prove" the thesis that socially undesirable qualities are not part of human nature, but the result of sabotage and infiltration by enemies and traitors.

3. The doctrine of socialism is not scientific but utopian. "Scientific socialism" distinguishes itself from other doctrines of salvation by claiming to describe objective laws of history. It asserts that "scientific insight" alone—not faith—is needed to enter into the earthly paradise of communism. Yet it requires terror and dictatorship to support its so-called laws of history, to show how humankind has inexorably moved toward a socialist utopia.

4. The socialist utopia is, without a doubt, a product of the contradictions of capitalism. The outrages of capitalism have not been resolved since Marx and Engels; in fact, they have worsened dramatically and on a global scale. Little is likely to remain of the "scientific" system called socialism; but of the anger and the criticism, the social and humanistic ideals that inspired Marx's revolutionary teachings, almost all.

We have returned to the beginning, we need a new critique. Those who would formulate this radical critique of capitalism must first drop the false intellectual propriety that says, "You have to know the answer before you can criticize." Who was the wise man who gave us the proverb: "He who says 'I know' has already stopped thinking"?

• • ◆ ◆ ◆

In Germany, Saigon Wins:
The Vietnamese in Berlin

On March 14, 1990, in West Berlin, an odd bit of theater caught the attention of passersby. A slender man was running southeast along the top of the Wall near Potsdamer Platz. He was traveling perilously fast, but then, when he stopped and crouched to jump, he suddenly turned and took off in the opposite direction. The scene seemed anachronistic. At first, witnesses thought someone was making a low-budget film about the Wall-jumps people had once risked their lives to carry out.

A second glance, though, revealed that the man on the Wall wasn't acting. A policeman ran like his shadow below, along the west side of the Wall. His uniform indicated he was with the East German border patrol. What moral imperative had driven this functionary to the western side? A few curious witnesses came closer. Now they noticed the unwilling performer wasn't German at all: his pale brown skin, his straight black hair, the shape of his face—all suggested he was of Asian origin. Who was being taken into custody, and by what right, the onlookers demanded to know. The soldier answered in breathless officialese: international accords required him to apprehend and return all fleeing Vietnamese.

During the ensuing argument, the refugee leaped into the West and shot off in the general direction of the Zoo. The border guard pursued him for some time, penetrating deep into formerly hostile territory. But he just wasn't fast enough. On his way back, he explained to the angry witnesses that he was under orders to bring those people back, even from the West.

For a moment, it seemed the clock had been set back half a year. The five exciting months that followed the opening of the Wall clearly had not happened for some residents of East Germany. Although it gaped with holes, for a pale brown minority in East Germany the Wall still meant what it had for over twenty-eight years to the bright-white population: the edge of the world.

The March 14 refugee was neither the first nor the last of his kind. In the days immediately following the opening of the Wall, dozens and then hundreds of Vietnamese presented themselves to the West Berlin authorities and asked for asylum. One by one, without passport or suitcase, they crossed the newly opened border, hiding in the westward-flowing human stream. Since the East German border guards kept spotting them and turning them back, many got through only on their fourth or fifth attempt. Social workers in West Berlin were at a loss. No one had expected these refugees, no one knew much about the nature of their residence in East Germany.

More came every day. By the end of May 1990, about 5,000 Vietnamese had fled East Germany, and most of them relocated in West Germany.

The mass appearance of "East German Vietnamese" in West Berlin was perhaps the most surprising of the many oddities that followed the opening of the Wall. People rubbed their eyes in disbelief: politicians, reception center personnel, even the press.

The basic facts were quickly established. In 1980, East Germany had signed an accord with the People's Republic of Vietnam which allowed skilled Vietnamese laborers entry and limited residence for purposes of labor. Under the terms of this agreement, thousands of Vietnamese came every year; by 1989, about 60,000 were employed in East German enterprises. That made the Vietnamese by far the largest single contingent of foreigners in a country not exactly overrun with outsiders—they accounted for well over a third of the 160,000 resident aliens. The accords prescribed a four-to-five-year commitment; after two years, the guests were entitled to a three-month home leave. Other than wages, the Vietnamese profited little by their residence in East Germany, for they were denied even the most basic civil rights. Their embassy took away their passports as soon as they arrived. They were housed in buildings resembling barracks where groups of seven were obliged to share "three-room apartments," completely isolated from the native population. They paid thirty marks a month per bed, low rent by Western standards (in Berlin-Kreuzberg, the welfare office pays rents that run as high as 1,000 D-marks a room). But by East German standards it was hardly a bargain: an East German citizen could get a three-room apartment of this kind for less than 100 marks.

In addition to rent and taxes, another reduction—"for the reconstruction of Vietnam"—automatically cut the salary of every Vietnamese worker by 12 percent. Rumor had it, though, that this money really went to pay off the Vietnamese Republic's debt to East Germany. Phrases like "loan worker" and "slave laborer" were on everyone's lips.

The hostel regulations were degrading; a hydra-headed security service made sure no movement went unobserved. The official guests couldn't even host their fellow countrymen from Karl-Marx-Stadt or Leipzig without advance permission; and Germans almost never came to visit. The security service also saw to it that everyone rose promptly in the morning and came home punctually every evening. Women could visit during the day, but the close quarters made for a generally monastic existence. Vietnamese women who got pregnant in East Germany either had to agree to an abortion or return home.

Amid these disturbing revelations, one historical curiosity went essentially unnoticed: weeks after the Germans staged their unification festivities, thousands of North and South Vietnamese celebrated a kind of mini-unification of their own. The exodus of Vietnamese to West Berlin provided a strange reflection of the German experience. Only gradually did it begin to dawn on Germans that Vietnam had also been a divided country for decades. Unlike Germany, divided west/east, Vietnam was separated into north and south. A Vietcong victory in 1975 had meant unification on the terms of the Communist North, but that didn't close the political and cultural gap separating the two halves. Millions of South Vietnamese preferred flight on the open seas to an enforced unification—hundreds of thousands died attempting to escape. Given their experience, it was inevitable that the Vietnamese in East Germany should have an especially acute sense of what German unification might bring. Many saw the unexpected collapse of the Wall, and of East Germany, as the utopian solution for their own country. A people that had been forced into a very unhappy unity looked on, breathless, as history showered its kindness on the German people. A worker I questioned in East Germany explained how the Vietnamese viewed German unification: in Vietnam, Hanoi had won; in Germany, Saigon.

Detlev Anders, of the German Red Cross, remembers vividly what it was like in the days following the arrival of these unexpected guests. At that point, three hundred incoming Germans were already housed on the city's fairgrounds. Acting on short notice, Anders and a few colleagues set up an additional 800 beds for the Vietnamese in the hallways of two of the buildings. Over twenty television teams announced plans to visit in the first few days.

As he led a camera crew into the building, he wondered for a moment whether it was last night's beer or a mild earthquake that was affecting his senses: the beds were rocking, softly but unmistakably; the German Red Cross blankets were moving rhythmically up and down. The camera people aimed their floodlights and cameras at the scene, but even the harsh illumination didn't quiet the localized tremors. "Cut," Anders yelled in desperation, blocking the camera and waving his arms: "Come back later." He was laughing, and the camera people laughed with him. In the nick of time, he came up with the one argument that could touch almost any German heart during those days: having lived in prison-like, monastic conditions for years in East Germany, the Vietnamese were celebrating their own reunification in the West. The footage never appeared on TV or even below *Bild* magazine's notorious four-inch front-page headlines.

Anders is the director of a Red Cross hostel in West Berlin. During the Vietnamese invasion of West Berlin, his most important associate was Jörg Flatow, from East Berlin, who has since joined the same organization as a social worker.

Anders and Flatow, each on his respective side of the Wall, had for years devoted themselves to caring for minorities in Germany; now the Vietnamese exodus brought the two men together. Some of the Vietnamese had come to Anders directly from Flatow, who had previously overseen the East Berlin Adalbertstrasse Transit Workers' Hostel. Then, in the summer of 1989, Jörg Flatow vanished from East Berlin. Three months before November 9 he had made a state-sanctioned visit to West Berlin and never returned. After November 9, he ran into one after another of his former charges in the West and so picked up his old line of work, only now on the West Berlin side and under the direction of his new boss, Detlev Anders.

The two men work closely together, and they get along extremely well. Within the microcosm of social work, these two men reflect a political division which also separates their North and South Vietnamese charges. Anders, coming from the "wild" West, is a skeptic, the ultimate inexorable idealist, while Flatow, who grew up in the "rigorous" East, emanates a cheery Mediterranean pragmatism. What the two share is a distaste for the superior attitude of the new German immigrants, and a sympathy for the not-so-white refugees.

"They're here barely two hours, they take one look around, and come back swearing about what a shithole it is, crammed full of Turks!" Anders says it's a good thing the East Germans were relocated to dormitories and hotels as soon as the Vietnamese arrived on the fairgrounds. It would have been impossible to prevent fistfights and knifings. The first night, he took the precaution of ordering the supervisors to take knives and similar instruments away from all occupants, regardless of skin color. The result was disgraceful. The guards patted their East German compatriots on the shoulder while carefully relieving the Vietnamese of their tiny fruit knives. A month and a half later, Anders had to confront the sorry fact that the people from the church weren't any better. He had contacted a number of congregations to arrange a Christmas celebration. They were all ready to help stage the holy day for the refugees from the East. But when they discovered that the recipients of their gifts were to be Vietnamese, their neighborly love abruptly vanished. Even the information that a good third of the Vietnamese were Christians didn't bring about a change of mind—or heart; all three congregations withdrew their offer. A few days before Christmas, Anders managed to obtain several thousand marks from the lottery administration—this time he remained vague about the nationality of the recipients.

Only the fairgrounds management was unstinting in its support—they actually donated a Christmas tree and a large movie screen.

The two Red Cross officials introduced me to a group of Vietnamese who had fled to West Berlin. We met around a circular table in a suburban Chinese restaurant. A dozen Vietnamese, some with wives and children, told me their stories. Contrary to my assumption, they had not arranged to flee as a group. "Every one of us has a different story, and we all have to decide for ourselves." They were all aware that the short trip to the West was a journey with no return. Because the Wall prospectors had turned the former border area into an immense excavation site, paths had sprung up leading through the wilderness. I learned that the Vietnamese travel a surreal route to the West that twists past abandoned watchtowers, in between clipped wire fences, and through holes chiseled in the Wall. West and East Berlin Vietnamese tread this route daily, trading news and probably goods as well: some call it the Ho Chi Minh Trail.

News matters most. Many of the refugees have families in Vietnam. When I asked whether their escape might cause problems for their dependents, most of them were confused or silent. Perhaps they really couldn't say, but I had the impression that they just didn't want to. They had no doubt, though, about what would await them if they ever returned to Vietnam. A few drew a finger straight across their throat; others put an imaginary gun to their head and pulled the trigger. "Dead," they said with a smile.

Going back to Vietnam was out of the question: "Only if they have a revolution like East Germany's."

These people had burned all their bridges. And the final decision to risk an escape and its consequences seemed to have had something to do with political geography. A quick poll around the table revealed that everyone except Tang, the interpreter, came from South Vietnam. Vu had a wife and son in Saigon—"Ho Chi Minh City," he added, in case I knew the city only by its new name. His father had been an attorney with the Saigon regime. In 1975, the "new regime" commandeered their house and sent his father to a reeducation camp near Saigon. None of the children were allowed to attend school, including Vu. He was drafted into the new regime's army in 1976. He was supposed to serve in Cambodia, but he deserted and hid out in Saigon. "After what they'd done to my family, I had no respect for the regime, I hated it." But Vu was caught and sent to a labor camp. From 1976 to 1980 he worked on sugarcane and pineapple plantations. For nine to ten hours of forced labor a day, he received food and enough pocket money to buy himself an occasional cup of coffee. He was then sent to another camp where he did forced labor until 1988. He was now thirty-five years old, and his health was ruined. All told, he had done twelve years of forced labor for deserting. He was now too old to work in East Germany—the negotiators had apparently established thirty-five as the cutoff point. But for good conduct and a bribe he nevertheless managed to obtain permission to come to East Germany. From the beginning, he saw the trip as a means of "escaping to a free country." By comparison with the People's Republic of Vietnam, East Germany seemed to him a paradise, "a free country, though still—unfortunately—a Communist country."

The other Vietnamese echoed this sentiment. Only when faced with the prison-like hostels and the increasing rudeness of shopowners did their positive picture of East Germany begin to cloud. More and more, the Vietnamese were treated like thieves, as if they were paying with money that wasn't theirs. Graffiti began to appear on buildings: "Up against the wall, Vietnam," or "Before a German has to leave, we'll throw out the Vietnamese." They no longer dared walk the streets after dark. While they remarked that xenophobia had increased exponentially since the opening of the Wall, all agreed that the officially proclaimed "friendship of the people" had been a total failure from the start: East German citizens made no connection between the catchphrase "heroic struggle of the Vietnamese people" and the actual Vietnamese who lived in their midst. No one, either at work or at the cultural centers, ever asked the Vietnamese about their lives in Vietnam. The East German hosts didn't care whether they were dealing with heroes or foes of "the people's anti-imperialist struggle." At best, what Vietnamese guest workers got from their German colleagues was the remark: "I've already done my bit.* Why should I fatten you up as well?"

These experiences may have strengthened the resolve to escape to the West, but they were not the deciding factor. Many Vietnamese had thought about fleeing even before they arrived in East Germany. Every story made it clearer: their experiences in South Vietnam had disposed them to join the exodus to West Berlin. Fear for their relatives at home was no reason to waver—over the past fifteen years they had already been exposed to every reprisal imaginable.

Finally, I couldn't resist asking a question that would also help me deal with my own political past. After fifteen years, I asked, how did they see the American war in Vietnam? "It was absolutely necessary," came the response. "The war against the Communists was a just war, and the Americans ought to have won. They pulled out too soon and like cowards." I couldn't hide my dismay. And what about the napalm, the bombing of Cambodia, the hundreds of thousands of people who had been ripped to shreds by American fragmentation bombs, the ecological damage that will linger for decades?

"It's true that the Americans and the Thieu regime also made serious mistakes," Tang agreed. He was the only North Vietnamese present, and it wasn't clear

* This refers to a regularly levied "donation" in support of "the heroic struggle of the Vietnamese people."

whether he was voicing his own opinion, or speaking out
of courtesy to me.

How did the other North Vietnamese who had remained
in East Berlin see these things? How did different life
stories from the North and the South affect the common
experience in East German hostels? Could two Vietnamese whose fathers had fought against each other really
get along, cooped up for four years in the same East
German room?

The Adalbertstrasse Transit Workers' Hostel lies right
by the Wall in East Berlin. Opposite it is a dilapidated
building covered with graffiti: "Resistance fighters West
and East, rise against the Nazi beast!" reads one. Another
calls for solidarity with Vietnam. It turns out the building
has been occupied by West Berlin *Autonomen*, a leftist
radical group. Other than this slogan harking back to a
distant time, there is no apparent link between the Berlin
revolutionaries and the Vietnamese workers. Unsullied
by cans of spray paint, the hostel entrance assaults all
comers with a barrage of German housemaster's bluster:
NO TRESPASSING. ALL VISITORS REPORT TO THE SU-
PERINTENDENT. IN THE INTEREST OF CLEANLINESS, NO
ONE MAY ENTER IN SOILED WORKCLOTHES. All neatly
painted on an enameled sign, along with: ENTRY
PERMITTED ONLY AFTER REPORTING TO BUILDING 60.

Jörg Flatow arrives, and his former charges give him
an enthusiastic welcome. The reason for his popularity
is obvious—he wasn't a stickler for the rules. Unlike
other overseers, Flatow repeatedly "looked the other
way"—he let visitors in unannounced, allowed people

to use his office phone, accepted invitations to dinner, and stood up to his boss. "No one's been that nice to us since," Tuan says. "Take my word for it!" Like the other 170 Vietnamese in the hostel, Tuan works for the Berlin Transit Authority. He himself is an interpreter, while most of the others are mechanics, fitters, and rail maintenance and yard workers. November 9 has left its mark here, too: there's more space. In the near future, the personnel will be drastically cut back, from seven "overseers" to two. Tuan notes this with satisfaction: "I've always said we're not savages, you can turn your back on us without worrying."

The Vietnamese had recently had their first informal meeting with the hostel director. Despite his usual strictness, the latter suddenly felt he had to confide to the Vietnamese that he'd been expelled from the Party in 1981. "That's a lie," commented Jörg Flatow with a laugh.

Tuan first came to East Germany in 1979 at the age of seventeen, and was trained as a computer and typewriter serviceman. His father works for the government in Hanoi, but Tuan had no idea what he really does. The only word he could find for his father's profession is "cadre." When I asked him if he thought of himself as a Communist, he replied that his father was a Communist and had influenced him a great deal. Tuan admitted that he was "very shocked" at first by the events of October and the bloodless revolution: "Why should these young people want something more? They already have so much!" But later, when he read in the papers about the corrupt East German leadership, he understood their reasons better. Now he's come to believe the young people were right and that Vietnam, too, ought to have more democracy. "But we're taking it slowly in Vietnam, not like here." Tuan first visited West Berlin on May 1, 1990. There was no border check at the Wall that day, but he's never thought about escaping to the West. "We have our wives and our children. We want to go back to our families."

He doesn't reproach his companions in the West, though, and continues to visit and write to them. "Most of them are South Vietnamese, and in the South people are more pro-West." He thinks the refugees' assertion that they would be shot if they went back to Vietnam is absurd. "That might have happened before, but we're living in a new age now." Tuan says he's never heard about forced labor camps. Still, he frowns on the power elite's tendency in Hanoi to refuse jobs and offices to South Vietnamese: "It's a social problem we've inherited from the past, but in five or ten years we'll be able to forget the past." In conversation, he favors the official "we," and his responses often sound canned. He talks like someone who knows that a careless statement could eventually come back to haunt him. Five months after East Germany's bloodless revolution, an invisible Big Brother was still sitting among the Vietnamese at my table, listening in. I wonder how Vu would have managed sharing a room in East Germany for two to four years with Tuan—the one having spent twelve years in work camps, the other not even believing that they exist. But is Tuan really saying what he thinks, and would he say it to a Western reporter? And hasn't Vu adapted his views as well, out of concern for the new Big Brother who rules on requests for political asylum?

Jörg Flatow takes me to another apartment on the third floor. Family photos decorate the walls, with a pinup here and there. The calendar girls who arouse the workers' fantasies are fully clad beauties with lotus flowers in their hair; in three-quarter profile, they favor their admirers with a shy smile. Two men lie on their beds watching a soccer game broadcast in French. Five others, who are gathered around a table, offer us a drink. Some of them were officers in Cambodia and in January 1989 they came straight from the jungle to the gray cement of Berlin. Now they're doing their four or five years with the Berlin Transit Authority for a grand total of 850 marks. "Not enough," they say. When the Wall came down, they shared the Germans' joy and excitement, but now they find more and more that they are outsiders in a hostile society. At work and on the street, the East Germans are abandoning all the courtesies imposed on them by the old regime. A short while ago, the home-leave policy for the Vietnamese was eliminated: one man, a doctor now employed as a mechanic, guesses it will be four years before he sees his wife and children again— will they still recognize him then?

It is now dangerous to leave the hostel in the evenings. Organized teenage gangs are out looking for trouble, and they always find it. Even the police have abandoned all restraint. Not long ago they randomly arrested a young worker from Haiphong on Alexanderplatz, took him to a police station, and searched him. In their opinion, he

was carrying too much cash—so they confiscated it. Even
Tuan, who never used to worry, is now reluctant to be
out on his own late at night. "We understood you," he
says to Jörg Flatow, "but you deserted us, you should
have stuck by us!" When I say goodbye, Flatow accom-
panies me to my car and then goes back into the hostel.

In the euphoria that followed the opening of the Wall,
the fantasy of freedom lasted only a few weeks for the
Vietnamese. How will a "Saigon"-controlled, united
Germany treat Hanoi's Vietnamese?

It looks as if, after their initial delight, the East German Vietnamese are going to remember the festivities
in honor of German unity as the sealing of their fate. So
long as there were two states, West Berlin and many
West German provinces offered asylum to thousands of
East German Vietnamese. But according to the Cap An-
amur Committee, a Vietnamese refugee organization,
East and West Berlin police secretly agreed, shortly after
the opening of the Wall, to return fugitive Vietnamese
to East Berlin. And in the Bavarian town of Hof, officials
put a Vietnamese woman who had requested asylum back
on a train for East Germany—without a hearing. Since
these measures violate the constitution of the Federal
Republic (any refugee who can show political grounds
has the right to a hearing), they were successfully challenged in court. But this legal protection vanished with
unification. Authorities who incline to deportation may
now take cover under a new state accord with Hanoi
negotiated by Hans Modrow's transitional government
in East Germany. Under the terms of this accord, the
Vietnamese government will recall all 60,000 Vietnamese

"guest workers" by 1995. Another clause specifies that any Vietnamese who are unemployed and can't find lodging or work on their own must return home within three months.

No one knows how the regime in Hanoi deals with Vietnamese who flee to the West. But the South Vietnamese I talked with didn't have to invent any threats; the reeducation and work camps still exist. But even the Vietnamese returning from what was once East Germany won't find it so easy to be back home. They have witnessed the democratic revolution in Europe, and now constitute a dangerous source of discontent.

And the Germans? Now that they're happily reunited, how will they treat their guests from the Third World who have shared the same divided fate—but without the happy ending? The clocks, it seems, are now being synchronized to Central European Time and mirrors only get in the way.

Two Successful Rogues

The scene looks familiar—it must be a play or a film about the Third Reich. But no, it's the television evening news, and the dialogue is definitely real and not invented. A defendant is talking to a judge—I know the lines by heart.

"Do you remember me?"

"You're . . . just a second . . ."

"Attempted flight from the Republic. You sentenced me to three years and—"

"That's right. In fact, I remember your case quite well, Herr . . . what was your name again?"

"Do you regret it now, that sentence?"

"Regret . . . You have to realize, there were no laws we had to uphold, and in the context of the time, the sentence was entirely correct."

It's not so much the judge's excuse that lingers in my memory; what continues to resonate are the words he didn't say, the one simple sentence he couldn't get past his lips: "I'm sorry, I did you wrong." He doesn't show even the slightest sign of compassion—after all, that would practically amount to an admission of guilt, an admission that might even be "admissible" in court.

On the strength of the code that maintained law and order in East Germany "in the context of the time," prosecutors and judges put about 200,000 citizens behind bars. Elastic clauses like "treasonable transmission of information," "agitation against the state," "obstruction of state or societal function," "conspiracy," or "unlawful border crossing" provided the legal instruments for state terror. Examples: A young man named Uwe Reimann was found guilty of "agitation" for distributing leaflets protesting compulsory military training in high school and college—two years and two months. Author Rudolph Bahro was found guilty of "treasonable transmission of information" for allowing his book *The Alternative* to appear in the West—eight years. Members of the Environmental Library were convicted of "conspiracy" for carrying a subversive poster alongside the official Rosa Luxemburg parade—six months. (The poster quoted Rosa Luxemburg herself: "True freedom means the freedom to disagree.")

Annulment proceedings are now under way to reverse about five hundred of the sentences pronounced as part of this legal terror, and its victims—mostly the prominent ones—are being rehabilitated. But what about the jurists responsible?

The task of sweeping out the East German judicial stable has been entrusted to the Ministry of Justice, the second most powerful instrument of political repression in the country after the Ministry of State Security (the *Staats-sicherheit*, or Stasi). Following Honecker's ouster, Kurt Wünsche became the new Minister of Justice. Wünsche had held this post once before under Walter Ulbricht in the heyday of Stalinism, succeeding the notorious Hilde Benjamin, who had initiated the first East German purge trials. The Citizens' Committees have shown that the plans for Stasi internment camps for "people who think differently" date from his tenure. It would have been a miracle if a minister of that ilk had spoken any differently than he did on June 10, 1990, at a convention of East German judges. In the glass-roofed courtyard of the East Berlin municipal courthouse, he reiterated his opinion that the overwhelming majority of East German judges should continue to administer the law: "Yes, absolutely, that's how it is, and that's where I stand," he proclaimed to the thunderous applause of seven hundred judges. He protested that "common criminals" and losing parties in civil suits were now "restyling themselves as victims" of political oppression, when according to his calculations only 1, or at most 2, percent of all East German court cases were "political." In the meantime, he reported, at least 5 percent of all judges had been forced to resign their office either due to their involvement with such cases or because of their affiliation with the ruling party. (The exact figure is seventy-eight—out of 1,300.)

German history apparently suffers from a compulsion to repeat itself. The first generation of judicial administrators in the Federal Republic learned and practiced their craft, for the most part, in the Third Reich. None of the approximately 1,000 judges who presided over the

Nazi "People's Courts" was ever convicted. One of the last proceedings against Nazi magistrates involved Hans Joachim Rehse, who, as judge of a People's Court, shared responsibility for sending 231 citizens to their deaths. The West German Federal Court found Rehse not guilty of murder. The grounds given for his acquittal prefigure the self-defensive logic used by the East German judge I had seen on television: Rehse's sentences were declared "within the framework of what was legal in the context of the time."

This juxtaposition suggests a cynical conclusion: Why should the juridical attempt to overcome the past fare any better in East Germany now than it did in West Germany years ago? Now as then, the enterprise seems doomed because of a lack of qualified jurists; after all, one can hardly expect those who administered injustice to pass judgment on themselves. Besides, there's a problem of legal philosophy. A polity which elevates the violation of human rights to the status of law can hardly use the law to prosecute those violations. This is true even if that polity incorporates into its constitution various internationally recognized principles and rights.

Which is what East Germany did, by adopting entire clauses from the accords of the International Military Tribunal at Nuremberg. In practice, however, these additions failed to offer the slightest protection against a legal terror that completely violated the Nuremberg statutes, both in letter and in spirit. A striking example is the case of Heinrich Toeplitz, the former president of the East German Supreme Court. In 1962 Toeplitz sentenced one Harry Seidel to life imprisonment for helping people flee to the West, citing article 6a of the International Military Tribunal: "continued violation of laws designed to preserve the peace." This same Toeplitz was recently entrusted with overseeing the commission assembled to examine corruption and abuse of office in East Germany.

To charge the leaders of the state with "abuse of trust" or "acts of disloyalty to the detriment of socialist property" was not only shortsighted; it was also senseless. Even if these accusations could actually be proved in one case or another, they miss the real point, which is to expose and prosecute a different type of crime. Of course Erich Mielke, the erstwhile head of the Stasi, could and should be called to account for violating articles 28 and 31 of the East German constitution, which guarantee freedom of assembly and the privacy of mail and telephone. But wasn't it his *job* to violate these articles, and does this violation fully describe his crime? The charge of "high treason" promises equally little success, for under East German law "high treason" is defined as a felony aimed "directly at the overthrow of the socialist state and society." The hope of indicting the very men who headed the socialist state for the intent to overthrow it is simply ridiculous.

Clearly the worst crimes of Stalinism in East Germany are precisely those that cannot be prosecuted within the existing legal system. If even the highest officials can hide behind claims that they were acting according to the laws and constitution of the state, their subordinates will not fail to follow them in this matter as well. Every defense counsel will claim his client was only doing what was ordained by the political leadership, that he was acting within the framework of East German law, a system that also thwarted any *recognition* of wrongdoing. Particularly the thousands employed by the Ministry of State Security will be able to testify that they were only doing their jobs, in the service of the state's largest employer. A person would need an extraordinary reserve of obstinacy to maintain an independent awareness of wrongdoing within such a gigantic apparatus. According to the estimates of a former officer, the ministry relied on the cooperation of about a million informants over and above its permanent staff of 85,000 and the 109,000 "freelancers" it regularly employed. This means that among the approximately nine million employable East German citizens, one out of every ten was a stool pigeon. With their help, the Stasi created over five million secret protocols. Another two million files covered West German subjects. (Hence the strong reaction from Bonn against attempts to make the files public.) Rumor has it that if all the files were placed end to end, they would run the exact length of the Berlin Wall.

Citizens' Committees initially considered sending each affected citizen his or her file, but then immediately dismissed the idea, for it turned out that nearly every one of the millions of files listed close friends and even relatives of the subject as Stasi sources.

They weren't always bona fide informants. Even unsuspecting people who merely joined a conversation over dinner, or who were convinced they were helping catch an alleged Nazi, are listed in the files as "source" or "informant." Thus almost every name in the country appears as either victim or perpetrator or both. "If all this gets out," said Christoph Hein, who served on the first Investigative Commission, "we'll have a civil war on our hands."

All of this explains Hein's own response to the question, "Would you want to read the file marked 'Hein'?" "No," he answered, "I don't want to know. If it turns out my neighbor was spying on me, how am I supposed to go on living next door to him? Do I have to move because I can't stomach him? Besides, it may not be true. Perhaps *he* is being slandered. Still, the thought would continue to nag."

Hein's fears concerning the extent of surveillance seem modest in the light of facts that have recently been revealed. Another writer from East Germany, Erich Loest, actually succeeded in getting a look at his file. It turns out he had been spied on from 1975 to 1983, when he left for West Germany. His activities over those eight years, down to the most intimate details, were chronicled in a "diary" whose scope exceeded all expectation: thirty-one volumes of 300 pages each—about three typewritten pages for every day. Paradoxically, the case of Loest demonstrates the degree to which the Stasi fell victim to its own spying mania, ultimately drowning in the material it collected. The monstrous mountains of files required so much time and effort to produce that the information itself could scarcely be read and evaluated, not to mention used. Many references to "negative-hostile elements" or "subversive activity" passed by without consequence for the people concerned simply because the mighty organs of security couldn't find the time to follow through. The state-sponsored surveillance of almost every citizen, almost as pointless as it was hideous, ultimately took on a life of its own; it only existed because it was already there. So now should this Pandora's box be opened or safely locked away? When hundreds of thousands of people are involved, it's tempting to erase all difference between victim and perpetrator and cover everything with a cloak of silence.

A frightening conclusion begins to emerge: the first postwar chancellor, Konrad Adenauer, himself free of Nazi taint, was right when he proclaimed that the new democratic society would have to be built with the help of the old Nazis since there simply weren't enough uncompromised people around. The appointment of Hans Globke, who had helped write the Nazi race laws, as Secretary of State was simply the unfortunate, extreme example of a principle that was basically correct. In the light of the difficulties now confronting the review of East German juridical transgressions, one is suddenly inclined to be more lenient when passing judgment on the earlier West German sins of omission. The reverse is true as well; after all, why should people be any more strict in 1990 than they were in 1945, when far more fearful crimes had to be atoned for? Detective writers have apparently overlooked the only truly perfect crime: the one in which an entire society is complicit.

Or perhaps two societies. For from both sides of the Wall a great coalition formed, of Silencing and Keeping Silent. The first democratically elected officials of East Germany were in complete agreement with their brothers in Bonn: the only option was amnesty—although the word has come to sound more and more like amnesia. There's little mystery as to why the top East German politicians chose this gentle solution. Consider the fact that each of the respective chairmen of three new parties had to step down because of suspected collaboration with the Stasi: Wolfgang Schnur, Ibrahim Böhme, and Lothar de Maiziére (who actually headed the government until December 1990). And just before his resignation, de Maiziére had to dismiss his Minister of the Interior, Peter Michael Diestel, because the latter couldn't resist employing former high-ranking Stasi, not only in his own office, but even in the Committee for Dismantling the *Staatssicherheit*. According to well-founded rumor, at least 10 percent of the East Germans now in the parliament—about forty people—were in the active employ of the Stasi. Naturally, not one has taken advantage of the opportunity to admit his own involvement.

Why their colleagues in Bonn are pleading equally energetically to forgive and forget can only be attributed to the deep empathy that comes of shared experience. Ever since the beginning of the Cold War, when the Allies entrusted the further prosecution of Nazi criminals to the two German states, the West Germans were largely successful in muddling the job. Out of approximately 80,000 proceedings initiated, only 6,215 resulted in convictions, and most of the actual prison terms ran from two to five years. The East Germans, on the other hand, fulfilled their task much more vigorously. Given this disgraceful imbalance, it's easy to see why few West Germans are anxious to flaunt their moral superiority vis-à-vis East Germany.

In fact, the Germans united on the question of guilt substantially more quickly than they did on the question of currency: long before the monetary union, they achieved a union of forgiveness. It should not go unsaid that monetary considerations influenced the issue of guilt, for if the new Federal Republic did assume responsibility for the trials of the perpetrators, it would also have to be prepared to cover the costs of damages to be paid the victims, currently estimated in the billions of marks.

And how to deal with all the hundreds of thousands of Stalinist collaborators? It seems the least conspicuous solution has won the most support, and the job of separating the black sheep from the dark gray, the spotted, or even the white ones is simply being left to regional administrations. Thus it will be up to individual West German officials to decide who among their East German colleagues is suited to serve in the new unified Republic and who isn't. Of all conceivable solutions, this has got to be the most arbitrary and unjust.

As far as public trials are concerned, all parties are in complete agreement: don't hold them. No one is qualified, they say, to pass judgment on the East Germans, for no one knows with absolute certainty how he himself might have behaved under similar circumstances.

In her book *Eichmann in Jerusalem*, Hannah Arendt harshly criticizes similar arguments invoked at the time of the Eichmann trial. "About nothing does public opinion everywhere seem to be in happier agreement, than that no one has the right to judge somebody else," writes

Arendt. "It is the sign of sophistication to speak in generalities according to which all cats are gray and we are all equally guilty."

The comparison between any actions against the "Stalinist perpetrators" presently under way—and already given up—with Adolf Eichmann's trial in Jerusalem is dangerous. Since the actual offenses being tried are so different—after all, unlike the Third Reich, East Germany did not systematically murder millions of civilians—any comparison could easily lead to a minimalization of Nazi crimes. Nevertheless, the analogy is practically inevitable, at least as far as the legal aspect is concerned: How can crimes that were committed without any recognition of wrongdoing and in complete accord with the laws of the state be prosecuted? Arendt described the difficulties of judging such "administrative crimes" in the Eichmann case. These crimes, she points out, "undeniably took place within a 'legal' order. That, indeed, was their outstanding characteristic."

Bringing a crime of this type to justice created a dilemma for the lawyers, the judges, and the philosophers of law. The time-honored legal principle *nulla poena sine lege* (no punishment without a law) had to be replaced with a new principle allowing for a "retroactive" law. Arendt herself came out clearly in favor of passing judgment *ex post facto* with the argument that "if a crime unknown before, such as genocide, suddenly makes its appearance, justice itself demands a judgment according to a new law." The new law used in Jerusalem derived from a concept that had been recently established by the Nuremberg Tribunal, the "crime against humanity." In this crime, Arendt argues, conscience and intent are not the issues. One fact alone suffices to send Eichmann to the gallows: that he "carried out, and thereby actively supported, a policy of mass murder."

While we are obviously not confronted with administrative mass murder in the case of East Germany, we are confronted with "administrative violation of human rights." And I would forcefully submit a plea for these crimes to be tried in public. My first argument is based on the general attitude of impunity among the perpetrators. Every henchman, torturer, and tormentor working for a totalitarian state is completely convinced that he can't possibly be brought to justice—either because he is protected by the orders of his superior or covered under the laws of his regime. Klaus Filbinger, the governor of Baden-Württemberg who was exposed as having been a Nazi judge, coined the classic formula for all such criminals: "What was right yesterday can't be wrong today." It is this surety of the perpetrator which explains the horrible solitude of the victim as every interrogation, every physical and psychological abuse begins with the tormentor's threat: "No one can see you here, no one can hear you, I can do whatever I want to you, I can even kill you—and no one will ever bring me to trial!" This cynical self-assurance, so often confirmed by history, must be shattered once and for all. Proceedings must be brought against the criminal officials of East Germany to show them and their sort that they will be held personally accountable despite their pedantic allegiance to orders and literal loyalty to authority.

I am also persuaded by a second argument for public proceedings, namely the principle articulated in Jerusalem that "justice must not only be done, but must be seen to be done." Clearly one cannot accuse or convict all the guilty parties. It has not been and will never be possible to convict all the Nazi criminals, and it has not been and will never be possible to bring all the Stalinist collaborators to justice. Nor is this essential. Any proceedings against the administrative crimes of Stalinism would transcend the mere meting out of justice to individual criminals. Just as every conviction of a rapist upholds not only the rights of the victim but of the whole community, so, too, would any public proceedings on the violation of human rights in East Germany be a "visible" vote of the community against future crimes of this nature. And this is not a practical matter of "prevention"—that word misses the point of such an undertaking. "No punishment has ever possessed enough power of deterrence to prevent the commission of crimes," writes Arendt. "On the contrary, whatever the punishment, once a specific crime has appeared for the first time, its reappearance is more likely than its initial emergence could ever have been."

Apart from the public rehabilitation of the victims, the effort to bring East German administrative criminals to justice would serve no practical purpose: it would simply announce the intent of a society to protect, under any and all circumstances, certain basic rules of communal human existence.

◆

Of course one may argue whether recourse to Hannah Arendt's concept of "administrative crime" is juridically productive. What is disturbing is that no one is doing so; the debate just isn't happening. But this much is certain: whoever tries to shirk the attempt even just to define Stalinist crimes in East Germany gets trapped in one rotten compromise after another. It is as dishonorable as it is ridiculous to charge those responsible for forty years of oppression in East Germany with "personal enrichment" or "embezzlement of public funds." The people's rage at the party bosses' extravagance, their luxurious Wandlitz homes, is understandable, but it would be deplorable if that's where it stopped. To pillory the leader of a police state because of central heating and a parabolic antenna seems to suggest insufficient or even manipulated information: every small-time shopkeeper in West Berlin lives better than that. The endeavors of the federal attorney in Karlsruhe to bring Erich Honecker to trial for "abetting a criminal organization" (the terrorist Red Army Faction) may look promising from a legal point of view, but morally this is the equivalent of a declaration of bankruptcy. Imagine: the head of state where sixteen million people were deprived of civil liberties is ultimately convicted for hiding nine or ten terrorists from the country next door. The logical consequence of such a verdict would be that the only victims of Stalinism were the West German antiterrorist squads.

The juridical attempt to overcome the past and actually deal with the history of East Germany must go further, even at the risk of raising objections to "retroactive" justice. Otherwise, people such as the following may well get off scot-free:

- The top judges and lawyers responsible for the legal terror directed against approximately 200,000 dissidents
- The Minister of State Security, the people who commissioned him, and the agents who helped him enmesh East Germany in a web of informers and spies
- The planners responsible for a system of at least twenty-four camps throughout the land, equipped with barbed wire and electric fences, for the internment of thousands of "parasites" and "unreliable elements"
- The doctors in Bitterfeld who knew as early as 1980 from a secret study conducted by colleagues in Rostock that local children were paying for the toxic wastes of a nearby chemical plant with incurable osteoporosis and various growth disorders—but who nevertheless hid this information from the children's parents
- The men and women responsible for decades of public misinformation in the media, whose "reportage" provided the ideological weapons used by Stasi interrogators and torturers in their daily work.

This list isn't arbitrary, just incomplete. Even if the guilty parties cannot be convicted in every case, it is vital for the political recovery of the community that the crimes be brought to public trial.

The question remains as to where such proceedings should take place, who should run them, and what should be their legal basis. Obviously neither East nor West but the newly unified Germany is the only conceivable venue. While the central judicial authority that will succeed those of both German states has yet to be named, it is likely that the constitution and legal code of the Federal Republic will prevail. I'm not convinced by the objection that it's pointless to have such "administrative crimes" tried by judges who already failed in the case of the Nazi criminals. That kind of thinking only expresses the solidarity of two successful rogues: "I won't tell on you if you don't tell on me." In fact, their previous failure might challenge the judges to make up for past mistakes. It wouldn't damage West German justice in the least if, in attempting to bring Stalinist crimes to justice, it had to review its own recent performance.

If. That's the conditional. The German indicative says: Let's forget it.

* * * * *

The Genealogist

If your name is Schneider (tailor in English), you aren't very likely to succumb to the allure of genealogical research. Instead of leading to one or two illustrious ancestors, such a name can only promise endless confusion with myriad other Taylors. I myself always felt the brothers Grimm had taught me enough about my name to discourage any further investigation. The picture of tailors that they stitched into stories is not exactly complimentary: the fairy-tale thimble masters are, without exception, show-offs and megalomaniacs. Never content with their lot, they are always striving beyond their reach. In fact, the only extenuating circumstance that might excuse this widely acknowledged character flaw is their work, for sew they must, twelve hours a day, in cold, cramped quarters. And it seems that in their exertions they forget about time and space and their station in life; as each stitch brings a new dream, tailors' minds wander with impunity. Moreover, they are always sewing clothes for clients from a higher class—rich merchants, noblemen, even princes—all of whom they have had occasion to see undressed. That's why tailors are the first to realize that clothes really do make the man. Confronted by aristocratic skin-and-bones and royal obesity that, unclad, would offend any mortal, the tailor must apply his art to create stature out of status, and furnish class with class. This intimacy appears to have promoted a second set of traits in tailors (apart from ambition and megalomania): they are alert, sly, adroit at deception, and endowed with tremendous reserves of humor. Sad to relate, they are also consumed by envy and easily blinded to reality, a hazard of the trade that can even lead them to commit an occasional murder. Invariably, however, it is their nature to pretend to be something better than they really are.

It would never have entered my head to resort to genealogy to verify this fairy-tale premise if a certain East German genealogist, named Marie Luise, hadn't pushed me to do so. Her own last name is as common as mine, and we're actually related, but so distantly that only she can explain how—I think that "great aunt by marriage" comes close to the mark. Several years ago she surprised me with a sample of her art. One or two shakes of my genealogical tree and down came a family legend involving a small painting that hung over our Bechstein grand piano ever since I can remember, a portrait of my paternal great-grandfather. (Or was it my great-great-grandfather? I have to ask Marie Luise.) According to an oft-repeated and eagerly heard story, he fought alongside Richard Wagner on the barricades in Dresden in 1848.

And while we, his great-grandchildren (or great-great-grandchildren) categorically refused to believe in inherited traits, we were inclined to make an exception in his case. By 1968 at the latest, we had come to like the idea of being genetically inspired by the rebellious forefather. Which is why Marie Luise's new critical edition of the family legend was such a shock. First, she expressed serious doubts as to whether Richard Wagner had ever even seen a barricade from any closer than the balcony of his luxurious apartment. Furthermore, she had documents proving that our ancestor had been apprehended as a revolutionary only by mistake, the unwitting victim of his own laziness. It seems that on the evening before the Dipoldiswalder rebels marched into Dresden, he and a friend happened to visit a tavern. Marie Luise told the story as if she had been there.

"Needles," the friend supposedly said, "let's make it easy on ourselves. I hear the tavern keeper is taking provisions to Dresden. Why walk tomorrow when we can ride along in his wagon tonight?" They arrived in Dresden late at night, in violation of the curfew, and were immediately arrested. My ancestor was accused of agitation and wound up losing his post as rector; for two years he also had to report regularly to the police. To his dying day he fought against the disgrace of being labeled a "Forty-eighter"—in vain. Presumably it was this injustice that led to his extreme hatred of soldiers, which he passed along to my great-grandfather, a pastor, and his three daughters, one of whom was my grandmother. As though to compensate me for this disappointment, Marie Luise offered me another finding from her research. Recently, quite by chance, she had stumbled across my mother's family while studying an armorial. It turns out that my mother descends from the nobility, and the trail could well lead to the highest aristocratic circles—but Marie Luise has to investigate further.

Oh, the wonders of genealogy! Still slightly dazed, I complimented Marie Luise on her accomplishment, but she only smiled modestly. It was as if I had congratulated an Olympic high jumper for clearing the bar at five feet. After all, it was purely by accident that she had strayed onto this subbranch of the family tree. And by the standards of the trade, even the lowliest apprentice could illuminate the deeds of an ancestor from the nineteenth century. True professionals don't really deserve to feel even slightly satisfied until they've reached into the seventeenth or sixteenth century. And the truly Olympic standard, the goal steadily pursued by every German genealogist, is Charlemagne.

Marie Luise confided this with downright disgust. She didn't care for Charlemagne, and didn't wish to descend from him or any other noble. Colleagues who set their sights on royal ancestors were suspect in her eyes. The most revolting example was an ancient lady, whose name Marie Luise didn't want to mention since she's a little too well known. At the founding of a genealogical association in Pankow three years back, amid the gathered descendants of Kepler, Luther, and Münzer, said lady lifted a dainty finger and proudly proclaimed, "And I am descended from the third marriage of Charlemagne."

The Genealogist

Marie Luise explains that then and there she took an oath: "Charlemagne—never!" Later she had to revise her historical distaste, but I'll get to that. In any case, she can't change the fact that the guild's highest laurels are reserved solely for those who can trace their trees to the time of the great Charles.

The hobby that Marie pursues has a broad and diverse following in East Germany; about two thousand organized genealogists meet regularly at conventions and conferences. In addition, there is an unknown number of amateurs independent of any organization. The clubs have existed since the mid-seventies; founded in the southern cities of Leipzig and Magdeburg, they have spread northward over the years. Also in the 1970s, a Central Office for Genealogy was established in Leipzig to prepare and issue standardized forms for the construction of genealogical tables. The completed tables are submitted to the Central Office, where they are sorted and compared with genealogical records already on file, and, when necessary, errors of tracking are noted. When Marie Luise handed in her own tree in 1985, it consisted of two thick volumes. The experts emitted an audible gasp and doubted they could turn up anything new. But eight weeks later she received twelve pages crammed with genealogical amendments. "When you suddenly discover that around 1600 you and Albert Schweitzer had common forebears, it's hard to be indifferent!"

The decisive clues, however, come from the lively written communications among the genealogists themselves. Guild members post letters more reliably than most lovers, always single-spaced on account of their length. The correspondents are bound by a spirit of mutual cooperation; they depend on each other. If one has just managed to trace his own tree back to the eighteenth century and in the process finds a document connecting someone else's tree to the seventeenth, he immediately shares the information. For by filling in a stranger's tree, the odds improve of eventually completing one's own. This sense of community does not stem solely from the gathering of kindred spirits, since the genealogists themselves are usually related to one another by blood, even if they have to go back twenty generations to find out how. Because naturally what genealogy ultimately proves is that everybody is cousin to everybody else, more or less—and practitioners often find themselves meeting in the same ancestral village. Does that mean that all Schneiders, Müllers, Schmidts, and Langes come from the same family? Marie Luise found the question amusing. "Now, really," she said. "Think about it yourself for a moment and you'll realize that can't be. Wherever a certain number of people lived together, someone had to mill and someone had to sew." But even this dilettantish question provoked some expert commentary. Apparently, a marriage between two unrelated Schneiders completely confounds the genealogist, by entangling family lines disastrously, inextricably. In fact, surnames themselves weren't used until the fourteenth century, as population density increased. Before that, families were named according to the property where they resided: the miller by the woods was called Woods. And, of course, it cannot be denied that every Taylor and Schneider family tree originally sprouted from someone who was, indeed, a tailor.

The main sources for genealogical research are the documents found in church archives and registry offices, since for the genealogist every life is built on four major dates: birth, christening, marriage, and death. Notarized documents didn't become obligatory until 1874; prior to that, such information could only be found in church records. Working with these sources, genealogists tend to develop peculiar historical preferences. For instance, Marie Luise has nothing good to say about Frederick the Great, whose armies rained so many cannonballs on Dresden and its churches that all the records before 1760 were rendered useless. She expresses similar feelings toward the Swedish regiments during the Thirty Years War, who wreaked such havoc in the villages that all sources before 1640 (or 1660) were destroyed.

Once I began to perceive the dimensions of this passion, I asked myself why it flourished so in East Germany. My immediate explanation was that a socialist society which postulates that all men are alike secretly produces the opposite drive, the repressed desire to be different. This phenomenon leads straight into genealogical research. What easier way for people to prove their singularity? By discovering that their chain of progenitors ultimately leads to a count, a king, or an emperor—or to a notorious criminal like Michael Kolhaas, or to great

scientists like Alexander von Humboldt or Adam Ries—
they are clandestinely, almost imperceptibly, suing for
a basic human right to be unique.

But it's a little more complicated than that.

Marie Luise began pursuing genealogy before the war.
She claims she inherited her passion from her parents.
Since all our common relatives—at least in the recent
past—may easily be traced to specific Protestant
churches, she has been in a privileged position as far as
sources are concerned. Perhaps as far as history is concerned as well. The Nazis' requirement that every German prove his Aryan lineage back to the seventh
generation provided her parents the impetus for further,
more serious study. Marie Luise calmly dismisses any
suggestion that the family hobby took its inspiration from
Nazi concepts of race. Actually, she adds, there's no
better cure for Aryan mania than serious genealogical
research. The Germans, in particular, prove to be a completely mongrel nation, a fact they apparently still don't
want to believe.

Then, too, on closer examination, it seems clear that
selfish, individualist motives alone cannot sustain the
hobby very long. The promise of an enriched identity
that genealogy holds out to the layman is quickly can-
celed by the sheer number of relations. When all the
descendants of Cranach and Luther who spend years of
research to be able to evoke these famous forefathers
convene at a congress, they are forced to realize that
they share the distinction with many, many others. Thousands or even tens of thousands may perch on the same
slender branch of a genealogical tree.

The Genealogist

As for Marie Luise herself, she has cleansed her passion of all selfish motives and now sets purely scientific standards for her work. While it's difficult to describe the joy she finds in her hobby, it's clear that it provides a detached yet completely personal access to history. For her, the medium of historical knowledge is not class or economics or some political event recorded in chronicles, but the person, or more precisely, the relative, who is, in turn, related to other relatives. And it's not just one's own family which thus becomes embedded in the great stream of social history: for every historical figure, Marie Luise can immediately devise flourishing genealogical trees, complete with children, aunts, great-nephews, and brothers-in-law.

Early on, while still a child, she had picked out three favorite historical greats: Ludwig Richter, Johann Sebastian Bach, and Martin Luther. Is she related to any of them? Marie Luise reflects on this question for some time before answering, finally, no. She is, however, related to a town scribe who had engaged in protracted juristic disputes with Luther. As always, her research led her to strange coincidences and chance discoveries. While she was tracing the scribe—and also following her husband's tree—she suddenly came across a certain Margarete Rössig. Just a minute, she thought, something's wrong here. Margarete Rössig is related to *me*, and now she seems to have married the wrong husband. Leafing further through the documents, Marie Luise discovered that the forebear in question was first married to her own ancestor and then to her husband's. "They must have had the same taste five hundred years ago as my husband and me," she said.

Despite this, she really doesn't believe in the power of genes, and even less in the various claims that people derive from them. As an example, she simply smiles tolerantly at the ancestral pride exhibited by certain Saxons. No researcher denies the fact that this particular branch of the German tree is very ancient. Its existence can be traced to the fourth century, and its written culture appears as early as 1330. Prussians, as well as Bavarians, have always been loath to admit how many "German" geniuses hailed from Saxony: Luther, Bach, Goethe, Nietzsche, to name a few. According to the Saxons, God placed the cradle of German culture in their bleak land.

What no one could predict, not even Marie Luise, was that throughout forty years of socialism, the Saxons would remain true to their Saxon king. In February 1990, while strolling through Dresden, Marie Luise and a friend discovered a brand-new Saxon flag bearing the old royal coat of arms displayed above a butcher shop. A seventy-year-old man passing underneath expressed his hope that the Saxon kingdom would at last be restored. The Prince of Saxony himself, he claimed, had already taken up residence in the Hotel Bellevue with his retinue and all his royal daughters, and soon everything would be the way it once was. Marie Luise's friend, also a genealogist and an expert on Dresden, immediately shattered the man's hopes. First of all, the Prince of Saxony doesn't have any daughters, royal or otherwise. Moreover, two of his three male descendants have no children at all and are too old and infirm to beget any. And on top of that, although the third does have descendants, he moved to Ireland to become a farmer, much to the chagrin of his family, who promptly disinherited him.

According to Marie Luise, the goal of the genealogist is not to restore former hierarchies of rule or ownership, but to investigate the life and times of a given ancestor. Recently, she phoned me from the West Berlin State Library. For days she had been poring over hitherto inaccessible folios from the earliest days of printing. When we met, she was still reeling from the shock of her latest discovery. She really couldn't help it, she never intended it, it all happened against her will—but there it was, scientifically indisputable. To her horror, she had just discovered a relative from the family Ahlenpeck. When she communicated her finding to the Central Office in Leipzig, a certain specialist there, well aware of Marie Luise's historical distastes, immediately burst out laughing. "Ha! Even you." Because wherever Ahlenpeck appears, Charlemagne is bound to follow. A distant relative named Hans von Landecker, Bastard of Ochsenstein, provided the link to the famous genes. He had married the Countess of Hesse, who, in turn, was directly descended from Charlemagne, so there was no denying the connection. And now Marie Luise, too, must come to terms with the ancestor she so steadfastly maligned.

Still, her knowledge protects her from false pride. For Charlemagne had seven wives, only four of whom were strictly legal. Six of these wives had children. Simple multiplication reveals a seven-digit progeny. Moreover, the noble blood has been thoroughly mixed: during the Peasant Wars, a number of Charles's descendants, no longer able to subsist off their lineage, married into simple artisan and peasant families, particularly in Bavaria, because only in the countryside was there enough to eat. As a result, countless sons and daughters of peasants can point to the legendary emperor as their ancestor, and they do. Yet it's somewhat of an exaggeration, Marie Luise adds, to claim that *everyone* in Germany is ultimately descended from Charlemagne.

I want to know exactly which of the four wives or three concubines was the grand matriarch of the clan. "I know for a fact," Marie Luise replies, "that I'm descended from Ludwig the Pious. And Ludwig is Charles's legitimate son!" Of course Ludwig didn't live much more piously than his father, and so Marie Luise's supposition that she likely inherited some traits from the illegitimate sons as well—by way of incest—cannot be easily dismissed. Her prime suspect is Charles the Bald.

She freely admits her relationship with Charlemagne has improved since the unwished-for discovery. In fact, now that she's related, she has begun to appreciate the many facets of his personality. For instance, his love of gardens—or else his idea of establishing schools for girls as well as boys . . .

Marie Luise shakes her head in mid-sentence and quotes a historian from the Roman period—with whom her relation is strictly spiritual: "Being proud of one's ancestors means nothing. What's important is to accomplish something yourself."

*   ◆   ◆   ◆   ◆

The Deep-Freeze Theory
and Other Hypotheses

I. Folk Music

On December 17, 1989, I lost confidence in my television's remote control device. It was 8:15 P.M., just after
the evening news on West Germany's ARD network,
and Alois Moig—all 200 pounds of him—appeared on
the screen in full Alpine dress, surrounded by a group of
Bavarian yodelers. I knew that if I failed to act decisively
I would face ninety minutes of German folk music.

By pressing the remote control button, I sought to
escape to East Germany's Channel 2, where I had often
found refuge from Alois Moig in Italian and French detective films from the 1960s. This time, however, I
couldn't believe my eyes: instead of Claudia Cardinale
or Gian Maria Volontè, instead of Simone Signoret or
Jean Gabin, who should appear on the screen but an
equally corpulent master of ceremonies, the spitting image of Herr Moig from the laces on his shoes to the collar
of his loden coat. The only difference was that the East
German program showed a marching brass band just

preparing to blast into their instruments as they thundered on stage.

"Ladies and Gentlemen, let's welcome the Black Pump Band from the local gasworks." The voice sounded a lot like Alois Moig. Or did he have a twin in the Erz Mountains whom the revolution had pushed into the spotlight? Back to the West German channel. There he was again, impossible to miss, the one and only Austrian original, Alois Moig—and in the middle of the marching musicians from the gasworks! "Stamp your feet and clap your hands, let's say hello to the Black Pump Band."

There was indeed only one Alois Moig, but was this his usual audience? Men and women ranging in age from forty to ninety were clapping and stamping along enthusiastically—but something wasn't right. Their hats seemed strange, their shirt collars all looked alike, and the material looked more like cheap polyester than cotton. Where was this program happening? As the camera panned the audience, I searched in vain for a clue. An East German friend had once told me that she could spot a "Wessi" by the lines around his eyes; it didn't work for me. I glanced at the TV listings, and only then did I realize that I had stumbled across the first united-German television broadcast, brought to us live from the East German city of Cottbus.

As the evening wore on, the program hammered away at the message: Music Knows No Borders. Thigh-slapping Upper Bavarians whooped it up to melodies played by industrial orchestras from Saxony, Swiss yodeling echoed throughout the Erz Mountains, cloggers from

The Deep-Freeze Theory and Other Hypotheses

Lower Bavaria stamped in time with Thuringian folk groups, while Alpine zither players vied with fiddlers from Mecklenburg. Whatever forty years of opposing educational systems had done to make the two German nations different, lederhosen, hunting caps, blond braids, and dirndls made them forget in minutes. The fact that Alois Moig reserved the name "German" solely for West German artists was discourteous but somewhat prophetic, and in any case it didn't detract from the general *Gemütlichkeit* in Cottbus. Any ill feeling disappeared as people locked arms and stamped their feet in four-four time. The Viennese participants added a touch of international flair with their apple strudel and the charming chorus: "We're all so young and oh so gay, come, so let us dance the night away." To wind up the evening, TV talk-show hosts from Austria, Switzerland, and East and West Germany joined one another on stage and sang: "East and West reach out their hands, and joy resounds from land to land."

Perhaps I should take a moment to explain my horror. I went to school in Upper Bavaria and learned to yodel at age six. While still a small boy, I was taught the *Schuhplattler*, the foot-stamping dance peculiar to that part of the world. At about the same time my father, a choirmaster from Saxony, introduced me to the music of Bach and Vivaldi, which I began playing on the violin. Growing up with Alpine horns on one side and a Bechstein grand on the other, I soon began to doubt the highly touted musical gifts of the German people. If a nation's musicality were judged on the basis of its folk and popular music, then we Germans would surely be among the least talented on earth. Our tradition knows no happy medium between serious and popular music. Unlike Verdi, Puccini, Bartók, Stravinsky, or Gershwin, our musical geniuses for the most part conceived their masterpieces in isolation, madness, and utter hostility to the composers of popular music. I myself know of no folk music more ponderous and less erotic than the oompah tunes of German folk festivals. They are felt not in the hips and pelvis, but only in the heels of the shoe; in fact, the only physical movement that the dreadful rhythm inspires is foot-stamping, which, as we all know, leads to marching.

II. Twins

I don't know whether the musical reunion of the two Germanys was transmitted via satellite to the U.S.A. It would certainly have met with professional interest in Minneapolis and St. Paul, because there, right in the Twin Cities, Dr. Thomas J. Bouchard has for the past ten years been conducting a study on twins. The legendary professor has taken it upon himself to solve, using exacting scientific methods, one of mankind's ancient puzzles: Is human behavior more strongly influenced by inheritance or environment? To my knowledge, the final results of this project, which Dr. Bouchard calls a "long-term study"—an extreme understatement—are not yet in. But some of the project's published case histories have already escalated the fierce war that has long been raging between the defenders of "nature" and the proponents of "nurture"—and driven the latter to despair.

For Bouchard's investigations have shown that identical twins, even when separated at birth and reared in totally different environments, exhibit personality traits that are similar to the point of absurdity. Even when kept apart by national borders, social status, opposing political systems, or oceans, these twins stuck to their inherited program, imposing it on their environment with inconceivable heroism. Deprived of all contact with one another, and often unaware of each other's existence, they smoked the same brand of cigarettes, preferred the same ghastly green suits, divorced their wives at the same age, and ultimately wound up living only ten miles apart, the white-haired schoolmasters of their respective villages.

The "Jim twins," Bouchard's most celebrated case, were separated at four weeks and raised in different Ohio cities. Thirty-nine years later, each brother had divorced a first wife Linda and remarried a Betty. Their sons were named James Allan and James Alan. Each had a dog named Toy and each had worked first as a gas station attendant and later as a sheriff's deputy. Each brother drove a Chevrolet, and each had a garden with a tree encircled by a wooden bench that he had painted white.

The German equivalents—the Hansel or Gretel twins—presumably exist, though they have yet to be documented. Even so, the behavioral scientists have their work cut out for them, for the area stretching from the Rhine to the Oder presents a vast laboratory—not exactly a voluntary experiment for the subjects, but a bonanza for researchers. Admittedly, the comparison with the American study is a little weak, since we're dealing not with a few pairs of identical twins but with millions of Germans who may or may not be related. Consequently, what the twin researchers call "the power of genes" must here be replaced by more nebulous nomenclature such as "tradition" and "national character." Even so, the opening of the Wall ended a unique social experiment which has yet to be described, not to mention analyzed. To put the question somewhat frivolously: What happens to a nation that has been split apart and brought up in two radically different schools for forty years? Which traits will prove resistant to change, and for how long?

As always, science will concentrate on the extreme test cases, the human subjects hitherto walled-in who were to become the New Man. And the data will either prove that nurture has indeed vanquished nature, or else it will show us a nation of sleeping beauties, spellbound for forty years inside their castle, now awakened by the kiss of unification, unaltered by a single day.

The question is not for Germans only; it concerns all the peoples of Central and Eastern Europe who, as a result of Hitler's wars, were forced to take part in the Great Socialist Experiment. How does a Pole from Warsaw, for example, communicate with his Chicago cousin after twenty or forty years of separation? Other, more distant (but also politically divided) countries like China, Vietnam, and Korea provide equally valuable material for investigation. A Hong Kong Chinese meets his uncle from Beijing in 1995 . . . or a Cuban boxer from the national team comes to conversational blows in a Miami bar with a former colleague now fighting for the Americans.

III. The Deep-Freeze Theory

Is it possible that some form of Communist "culture" really does exist, which, under the proper circumstances, might outlive the actual political and economic system? For years the experts have been offering two diametrically opposed hypotheses, essentially variations of the nature versus nurture debate.

The first of these might be called the deep-freeze theory. Simply put, it maintains that communism has "frozen" the historical peculiarities and passions of particular nations. When the freezer is defrosted, these people will take up exactly where they left off—in this case, forty-five years ago. All the lovely virtues and victories of socialism that were poured down their collective throat at thirty degrees below zero will melt away like snow in the spring. National traits both good and bad—acquired over the course of history—will revive as fresh as the day they were frozen and once again determine the behavior of the tribe.

The champions of nurture bitterly oppose the deep-freeze theory, insisting that social experience (even the impoverished Communist one) shapes people at least as much as any "hereditary" tradition. Forty years of different schooling must have left a mark on its pupils.

Until now, these questions have remained purely speculative, for lack of access to the subjects. However, since the opening of the Berlin Wall, preliminary observations have been recorded, and they seem overwhelmingly to favor the deep-freezers. One East German citizen in particular has set the pattern for the rest of his compatriots. On August 12, 1961, he had borrowed three books from the American Memorial Library in West Berlin. The next day his government erected the Wall, which afforded him ample time to read but, alack, also caused him to miss the due date. The first thing this faithful book borrower did when the Wall opened up was make his way to the American Memorial Library, where he returned the books, on November 10, 1989, in excellent condition, twenty-eight years late.

Other nations beyond the Wall also present overwhelming proof in favor of the deep-freeze theory. As though only a day had elapsed since 1945, national passions and rampant nostalgia are bursting out all over Eastern and Central Europe. The Polish eagle has again donned its ancient royal crown, though at the moment there's no money for the gilding. The old flags and coats of arms are also making their reappearance in Czechoslovakia, Romania, and Hungary, as the prefix "People's" disappears from the names of the various republics. The citizens of Karl-Marx-Stadt again call their city Chemnitz, and the countless Lenin Avenues and Karl Marx Boulevards are reverting to their former names. Where will the revisions stop? Will Gorky Place, Bertolt Brecht Square, and Rosa Luxemburg Street survive? Will homage again be paid to bygone tsars and kings, their long-neglected queens and loyal generals?

In any case, it's an expensive transformation: the emblems above countless entrances, the insignia on hundreds of thousands of uniforms, the portraits on millions of stamps must all be changed. Evidently the people so impoverished by communism have no objection to spending whatever money is necessary to restore their national identity, even if such expenditures won't fill a single belly.

There are other, far more alarming signs that support the deep-freeze theory. Forty—or even seventy—years of indoctrination in "proletarian internationalism" have obviously had little impact. Everywhere east of the Wall, minority groups nearly forgotten in the West are suddenly making themselves heard: Albanians in Yugoslavia, Slovaks in Czechoslovakia, Hungarians in Romania, Turks in Bulgaria. And everywhere they meet the same response, as fresh-frozen nationalist and racist resentments thaw, potent as ever, to the surprise of both Western observers and Party ideologues. Romanians who suffered silently for decades under Ceaucescu's tyranny turn around and bloodily vent their fury on the country's Hungarian, German, and Gypsy minorities. The nationalist fever also rages fiercely in the Soviet republics, where even women, children, and old people are beaten to death solely because they belong to another tribe.

A new wave of anti-Semitism is breaking across the old continent. In Poland, the church, which had kept silent far too long, saw itself forced to distribute a pastoral letter in defense of Jews. In the Soviet Union, every week sees the exodus of thousands of Jewish refugees, who are being threatened quite openly with pogroms by right-wing extremists and racist journalists. This threat is so great that some Russian Jews are seeking shelter in the land that organized the Jewish genocide half a century ago. Between May and December in 1990 alone, 2,000 arrived in Berlin. Nor is Germany—particularly the Eastern portion—free from anti-Semitic excesses, committed for the most part by young people.

In fact, it is in the former Democratic Republic that the outbreak of such sentiments is particularly noteworthy, since the Workers and Peasants State always proclaimed itself the very model of socialist internationalism. In May 1990, six months after the peaceful revolution, several newspapers ran a photograph showing dark-haired foreigners: men with sunglasses and hand-knit jackets, women wearing scarves around their heads and carrying children, all crowded on a narrow railway platform beside a train in East Berlin. Their eyes have disappeared in the shadows of the black-and-white photograph, and their faces speak of helplessness and despair. A tiny roof of prefabricated concrete hovers over the group, more a symbol of shelter than a real source of protection for the travelers, who seem on the verge of plunging onto the tracks in the foreground. The caption identifies the people as "Sinti and Roma," i.e., Gypsies.

For any German with a memory, this photo is a painful reminder. At first glance it's unclear whether it was taken recently or some fifty years ago: Have the Gypsies just arrived or are they being rounded up for departure? After all, such scenes are common in documentaries about the Third Reich when the Nazis herded hundreds of thousands of Gypsies onto the very same platform to be shipped off to the death camps. The accompanying text makes it clear we're dealing with new arrivals from Romania: so these are the children of the victims now crowding into the land of their parents' murderers. For the children of the perpetrators, this is an opportunity, a chance to make a historic gesture, a chance to implement true internationalism by flinging the doors wide open and finally welcoming these Sinti and Roma unconditionally.

But such gestures are the exception. Red Cross volunteers, refugee authorities, and church groups working around the clock struggle in vain against the sentiment of the majority who feel no pity for these people. At the same train station in the photograph, and at others, Germans stare with open hostility at the dark-skinned refugees from the East, even though millions of their own friends and relatives have sought refuge in the West. Those not content with staring use their fists. Local bars resound with language taken straight from the Nazi lexicon. And these passions have the blessing of the government. Peter Michael Diestel himself, the former East German Minister of the Interior, disapproved publicly of the foreigners' "undignified appearance." Travel restrictions were hastily enacted: as of May 18, 1990, only those Romanians who could prove they were tourists were allowed to enter East Germany. "Is the German Democratic Republic erecting its own Iron Curtain against the Romanians now so much in need?" asked Gerd Poppe of the liberal Berlin Alliance 90. His question will also fall on deaf ears in the Western half of the city, where the Social-Democratic City Senate has led the struggle to establish a coordinated "Entry Union" which would stop the flow of unwanted aliens into Western emergency shelters.

IV. Begging to Differ

However one evaluates the process of reunification, what's truly astonishing is not the resilience of the East German identity but the rapidity of its disintegration as citizens shed decades of indoctrinated behavior at breathtaking speed. All the advocates of an independent East German identity—myself included—did not foresee, and really didn't want to see, the extent of the general breakdown. The collapse of the East German economy only underscored what little reason East Germans had to preserve their identity, and so long as the comparison with the West is limited to the question of economic achievement, no one can argue with the pat assertion that the Great Socialist Experiment was just One Big Mistake. Anyone who still insists on basing his East German identity on the "superiority of socialism" is knitting his own foolscap.

Similar observations led Aras Ören, a Turkish poet living in Berlin, to a disturbing question: "Isn't it possible," he asked, "that a major crisis could cause West Germans to forget four decades of democratic indoctrination just as quickly? Who's to say that, under stress, West Germans wouldn't discard their democratic virtues with the same alacrity as their Eastern relatives are abandoning their socialist ones?"

I was speechless. Finally, after some consideration, I ruled out that danger. There is, after all, a fundamental difference between habits formed in a capitalist democracy and those that emerge in a socialist dictatorship. Even when it is imported from abroad, as in West Germany, democracy ultimately requires the consent of the governed if it is to survive. A socialist dictatorship, on the other hand, has no need of such consensus—even if it originated in an authentic revolution as in Soviet Russia. In fact, it is neither dependent on the consent of its citizens nor subject to their critique. The sudden and almost complete disappearance of all traces of socialism as practiced in Central and Eastern Europe is primarily due to the totalitarian form of the experiment.

"Democracy won't be shaken off so easily," I said, "because the people accept it and support it."

"Only because it's successful, and only so long as it stays that way," replied Aras Ören.

This dialogue led us back to the battle between the deep-freezers and the defenders of environmental influence. Against objections such as Ören's, that the authoritarian German character may thaw regardless of environment, the nurturists claim that a totalitarian state is not a bona fide environment to begin with: *any* East German Jim raised under Stalinism would come flying to rejoin his West German twin at the first opportunity. In fact, not only identical twins, but all sorts of friends and relations would behave exactly the same way. This is so predictable it is scientifically insignificant. Objective analysis of the Socialist Experiment, say the nurturists, neither proves nor disproves their theory. It only shows that people who have been tyrannized by something new will return to their old habits when given the chance.

And yet, as Christa Wolf has pointed out: "You can't just throw away forty years of life." Her cautious, purely descriptive sentence reveals what the simple economic comparison overlooks. Forty years don't vanish overnight solely because they were disappointing. Life was still lived in East Germany, even if the bottom line shows nothing to recommend the system. So what if socialism brought only negative experiences, they were still experiences. And if a year from now the pollsters and sociologists find East and West Germans to be exactly alike, this would not mean that no difference existed between the two cultures, it would only suggest that the difference had been suppressed.

At a panel discussion in East Berlin entitled Cultural Perspectives on Unity, I jotted down part of a sentence. It was spoken by a fifty-year-old woman in the audience who began her contribution by saying, "While I was still an East German citizen . . ." It wasn't the fact that she was accelerating the demise of the socialist state that astonished me—after all, it was May 1990, five months before unification. But how was it possible, I thought, to discard an identity that took over forty years to develop, as if it were merely an outdated passport? The audience, too, seemed interested in that question and soon joined in the debate. A sixty-year-old gentleman who introduced himself as a professor agreed with the woman, claiming, "I never actually considered myself an East German anyway—I was always just a German!" His statement provoked ironic compliments from people in the audience who congratulated the man on his achievement—for forty years he had managed to stay immune to his environment. Presumably he had pulled off the same trick during the Third Reich: so the only time he could have lived as a "real" German would have been before his birth. Konrad Weiss, another member of Alliance 90, answered the professor in a calm, unassuming, yet determined, voice: "I myself will be an East German for the rest of my life."

At that moment a man from West Berlin introduced himself as a teacher of religion and took advantage of the opportunity to deliver a brief sermon. For five minutes he enlightened his East German audience about the achievements of socialism and called on them to be proud. They answered with courteous silence: some stifled their laughter by coughing, others pretended to sneeze. Konrad Weiss again broke the tension by saying, "I suppose we're a little too tired to listen to missionaries from the West explaining our lives to us."

Then it was my turn, and I decided to risk a few of my own cherished ideas about the differences between the two German cultures. My reception was little warmer than the religion teacher's; I unwittingly managed to alienate both sides. "After all these years," somebody said, "we should be emphasizing the similarities, not the differences." A discreet gesture from the panel let me know that they didn't want to hear such ideas from a Western observer fortunate enough to have been spared the East German experience.

It wasn't the first time I had run into "misunderstandings" of this nature. When discussing the differences between Germans East and West, it really does matter who is speaking, and in what tone of voice. Western observers are generally inclined to address the differences, which, point for point, invariably demonstrate Eastern inferiority. No enthusiastic *"vive la différence!"* can compensate for what is quickly perceived as condescension. The East Germans have learned that their Western cousins profit from the difference, while they are bound to suffer from it. In an ideal society, in which all are equal, difference might be enjoyed as diversity. But as long as difference favors the person pointing it out, there's always the suspicion that by citing it, that person just reinforces his advantage.

The difference most stressed or denied by East and West Germans is their approach to unification. While the East Germans have been strongly pushing for unity ever since the Wall opened, West Germans have been content merely to respond to Eastern demands. And even this echo gradually diminished in volume, as the projected price of unification rose from month to month. When the first opinion polls in the fall of 1989 showed 80 percent of West Germans in favor of Kohl's rapid course toward unification, no one was asking the same people how much they would be willing to pay for it. When this question was finally posed ("Would you personally be ready to make some financial sacrifice for German unification?"), 61 percent answered yes in March 1990; two months later, the number had shrunk to 28 percent. Moreover, by spring of 1990 two-thirds of the citizenry found the tempo of unification "too quick," and the defeat of Kohl's own party in the parliamentary elections for Niedersachsen and Nordrhein-Westfalen was interpreted by most observers as the electorate reaching for the emergency brake. Since then, this West German trend toward sobriety has stabilized. The party at the Wall on November 9 left a hangover that will probably last for several years.

The general problem of difference, as revealed by specific differences concerning unification, is enough to drive both the advocates of environmental influence and the deep-freezers batty, for each side of the theory can look to only one side of the Wall for proof. The deep-freezers point to the Saxons, who, barely defrosted, their lips caked with forty years of ice, are again singing the stridently nationalist anthem, "Deutschland, United Fatherland." The nurturists counter that the reason West Germans have evolved beyond such nationalist passions has to do with the sunny climate of the free market economy.

The reunion party has been held, but it seems that the two German relatives are still passing one another by, as if they lived in different times as well as different places. While one managed to keep his traditional German traits intact by storing them in the socialist deep-freeze, the other lost his under the stimuli of the Western climate.

The whole thing sounds a little like science fiction, something out of Stanisław Lem: after an absence of forty years, a visitor from the East—looking not a day older—knocks on the door of his West German brother. The latter opens the door; his hair has turned gray, his face is drooping with age, and he wonders why his brother seems untouched by time. But after a while he realizes his first impression was misleading. Because his brother from the East has also undergone a change, an inner transformation. Time passed differently under socialism—but even if it passed more slowly, it did not stand still. Or in the words of one East German: "The deepfreeze itself was our environment."

V. *Homo Germanicus Orientalis*

Cold or not, the socialist environment definitely influenced East Germans in the area of antifascist reeducation. From the inception of the East German state to its demise, antifascism was official doctrine, and there can be no doubt that East Germany led in this particular race—even Western historians concede that the founders of the German Democratic Republic took their duty far more seriously than their Western counterparts. The fledgling state removed former Nazis not only from positions in government and education, but also from the courts, the post office, the state railroad, official medical associations, and, above all, from positions of leadership in industry and commerce. The West German press played up the exceptions—East German officers or state prosecutors with a Nazi past—but mostly to excuse Bonn's own inaction in this area. Besides, such cases in no way diminish the East German accomplishments. It wasn't by accident that the first years of both states witnessed a curious cross-migration at the German-German border. While most antifascists, old and young, viewed East Germany as their political homeland, the Nazis then residing in the East invariably moved west. Men like

The Deep-Freeze Theory and Other Hypotheses

Globke, Lübke, Kiesinger, Schleyer, Chapeau-Rouge, Rehse, and countless others painted a rosy picture for their colleagues left behind in the East: even ranking members of the SS or longtime Nazi Party members could achieve positions of honor and influence in the West.

One cannot quibble with the fact that the East German government managed to completely recast the old apparatus, often at great cost, since many of those dismissed were far more skilled than their replacements. What is problematic, however, is that from the outset, this housecleaning was performed to the accompaniment of ideological music. By 1949, the task of *Vergangenheitsbewältigung*—overcoming the past—had already been completed, according to article 6, paragraph 1 of the East German constitution, which declares: "The German Democratic Republic has . . . rooted out and destroyed German militarism and Nazism." Such instant success could be achieved only by bureaucratic fiat: anyone who joined the ruling Communist party was automatically clean. Carrying a party card became a substitute for the more laborious work of self-examination, remorse, and mourning. "The decisive factor is present political stance, not prior organizational affiliation," went the party line. As the economic disparity between the two Germanys grew, the antifascist refrain became the prime raison d'être of the Eastern state, and evolved in time into a full-blown historical lie that claimed antifascist resistance was strong in East Germany even *before* 1945. The Nazi monster had, miraculously, stopped at the Elbe. Although it was never stated quite so bluntly, many

East German citizens—particularly young ones—believed this fiction, thanks to the government's subtle deception.

For instance, on September 1, 1989, East Germany's Channel 1 announced the following: "Today is the fiftieth anniversary of the German imperialist invasion of Poland." Now, for forty years the word "imperialism" had carried the tacit prefix "West German." And since East Germany was the official "home of antifascist resistance," a younger viewer could only conclude that the invasion of Poland had been a West German enterprise. The success of such historical manipulation was proven by high school compositions commemorating May 9, 1945, the end of the war in Europe. A majority of the pupils expressed the conviction that on that day East German troops had fought alongside the Red Army to liberate Germany from Hitler and the fascist yoke. Unlike other items on the socialist agenda, this historical revision actually took root among the populace. For the government's need to legitimize its own educational dictates coincided completely with the citizens' need for exoneration from historical responsibility. Add to this a kind of "Hiroshima effect." The genocidal bombing of Hiroshima and Nagasaki had transformed the Japanese into victims, and they no longer wanted to hear about their own complicity in starting the war. Similarly, East Germans were transformed into victims by the Soviet occupation. Whatever role they may have played during the Nazi years was atoned for by their sufferings under Stalinism. Unlike in West Germany, the perpetrators had become the victims, and that's how they saw themselves. And this sentiment was shared by dissidents and party functionaries alike: whoever stayed in the East had chosen the harder lot, what Christa Wolf called "the tougher, rougher life," what Wolf Biermann described as "the better half."

Enter the German with a Clear Conscience. The conscience that ten years ago inspired the East German defense minister to offer, without a thought to the past, his Soviet friends the use of the People's Army "to restore order" in Poland. The conscience that allows some new arrivals to run around West Berlin venting their distaste for Poles, Turks, and Gypsies so shamelessly that many West Germans must envy them. One of the most important achievements of Hans Modrow's transitional government was that it broke with this tradition of a false clear conscience—at least officially. In February 1990 Modrow wrote to the World Jewish Congress acknowledging "the responsibility of the entire German nation" for crimes committed against the Jews.

No one would maintain seriously that West Germans have spent the past forty years wracked with guilt over their Nazi past. But the assertion that the past had been overcome, and that fascism had been "rooted out and destroyed," could never hold for very long in West Germany—if only because it could be so easily disproved. Far too many Nazi judges, doctors, and professors continue to enjoy their pensions undisturbed in West Germany. Every attempt to lessen the guilt—including Ernst Nolte's thesis that National Socialism was not unique in its essence, and Helmut Kohl's "grace of a belated birth"—has backfired and triggered strong protests in the press at home and abroad. We thus come to the peculiar conclusion that although the Federal Republic never broke with the past as radically as did the Democratic Republic, it was also less able to suppress it.

Thanks to its geographical location, West Germany received yet another benefit: the democracy imported from the Western Allies provided the Federal Republic with the opportunity of dismantling what was probably its worst historical inheritance, the "authoritarian character" made famous by Theodor W. Adorno and Max Horkheimer. Apart from any follies the student movement of the 1960s may have fostered, it at least broke with the past by introducing the principle of civil disobedience into an overly dutiful West German democracy. It is significant that the East German writer Heiner Müller sees the student rebellion of 1968 as an uprising "in the service of industrial capital"—the hedonism it advocated simply created new markets within the consumer society. Although Müller's reputation is that of someone who transcends borders, floating high above both systems, this analysis proves how firmly rooted he is in East German political soil. There the cult of obedience, which the Nazis had developed to the extreme, was taken over virtually intact by the socialist dictatorship. Thus East Germany has no experience with any form of democracy, and many intellectuals regard it with utter contempt. The authoritarian legacy suffered its first defeat during the 1989 revolution, and it remains to be seen how vital the new order will be. A few months of grass roots democracy are up against several decades of dictatorship.

Among the more short-lived traits of the East German species that are prized primarily by its Western admirers is the so-called "culture of the little niche," a nostalgic, if apt, description of a number of wholesome, neighborly virtues found in East Germany. "Helping your neighbor," "human warmth," "what you achieve is not as important as who you are," "friendship still counts," "things just move at a slower pace in the East"—all these phrases describe life in the little niche. One of the most notable successes of East German educational dogma is due to a paradox: the system actually did foster many of the proclaimed socialist virtues, though indirectly and against its will, the result of collective resistance to an all-powerful but economically inefficient state.

The East Germans themselves don't recognize these traits born of privation until they experience their absence, in the West. Then, suddenly, they're disturbed by the coldness of a society based on competition, by the emptiness behind the glitzy facades, by the general lack of consideration and the pervasive materialism. But this culture shock is becoming less and less intense as East Germany loses more and more of its identity. The virtues that sprang primarily from failure and need are, unfortunately, disappearing as quickly as the circumstances that created them. It's not uncommon to see people perform complete turnarounds. More than a few East Germans who have subscribed to the official picture of a "heartless" West are now seeking their salvation in success—at any price. Westerners try in vain to explain to them that even in capitalist countries it's possible to find a human being now and then. A former East German citizen who's lived in West Berlin for well over ten years and now runs into whole herds of his erstwhile countrymen as they stampede down the streets and into the stores of the city has concluded that East, not West, Germany was the true cradle of the "elbow society."

Another peculiarity of the species, also arising from historical disadvantage, will undoubtedly prove far more resilient and resistant. The end of World War II imposed unequal economic burdens on the two German states, and East Germans are now demanding the accounts be balanced. While some East German historians have recently quantified the difference, suggesting sums as high as 650 billion marks, the general populace is expressing its own demand for compensation in a widespread pattern of behavior that's become known as "entitlement assertion." This is making West Germans increasingly uneasy, and they are reacting—with contempt.

West Berlin taxi drivers complain about East German passengers who offer the following pitch instead of payment: "Hey, come on, I'm from the East." The proprietor of a bar reported that large groups of East Germans clad in the notorious stone-washed jeans wanted to pay their tab with: "How about making it on the house, we're from over there." In the first weeks after the Wall came down, West Berlin's retired population looked on with envy as their counterparts from the East rode buses and subways for a mere wave of their blue passport. (These passports, in fact, suddenly became a black market commodity: for about seventy-five dollars "Wessis" voluntarily became "Ossis" in the hope of obtaining a year's worth of free municipal transportation.)

Even well-to-do West Germans felt compelled to expound on problems which were not exactly existential. Mercedes drivers were angered that they had to pay towing costs for their illegally parked cars, while East German Trabants remained untouched. Sales managers grumbled about the "museum pace" of clients from the East who reverently beheld the merchandise instead of buying it. And the famous "rubble women," wearing diamonds on the same hands that once helped clear the bombed-out cities, invoked those glorious days after '45: "We had to start from the ground up too, and without any help from anybody!"

But pride in their own productivity didn't stop West Germans from invading towns just across the former border and cleaning out the stores with Eastern marks acquired on the black market. The *Frankfurter Rundschau* reported one such incident: "East German housewives from the town of Grevesmühlen looked on in dismay as a woman from the West entered the local butcher shop and bought up twenty of the twenty-one ducks for sale." The lines formed by Easterners in front of the cheapest Western discount stores corresponded exactly to those formed by Westerners in front of luxury restaurants in the East, where they could dine on roasted pheasant for only a few West German marks.

Here two incompatible versions of postwar history collide. The conflict is preprogrammed and sure to continue well into the future. While the West German says: "After all, I earned this with hard work," the visitor from the East holds out his hand expectantly, with the reply, "You were just lucky," and hopes for a private contribution to the "balanced burden." The conceit of the first is that his success is due solely to his own industry, while the second would like to think that the only difference between the two is a matter of luck.

VI. *Anecdotes and Antidotes*

For Germans from both sides, "efficiency," "industry," "honest acquisition," and "just deserts" are no joking matters. The story of an East German baker has become a Western classic. In the middle of a job interview the man discovers that the West German bakery never runs short of flour. He stands up immediately and walks out, unwilling to give up his accustomed "supply breaks." The sophisticated manipulation of information in the West furnishes a statistical "backbone" to such anecdotes. According to one poll, two-thirds of West German employers have noticed "certain deficiencies" in the new arrivals such as "poor performance," "poor teamwork," and "poor motivation"—figures, of course, were supplied to document each category. Further complaints concerned their refusal to work overtime, a tendency to tire early, and the "lack of any respect for deadlines." That there are actually eight hours in an eight-hour day seems a novel idea to East German workers, who furthermore seem "inclined to take unauthorized breaks." In Darmstadt, the employment office is offering "motivation courses" to new arrivals in which students practice "punctuality and responsibility."

The woes of Western employers are echoed in chorus by the Eastern employees, who complain about the "inhuman pace," "demeaning treatment," and "rude atmosphere." Used-car dealers have already gained notoriety for dumping their lemons in the East—at fantastic prices. Another Eastern classic tells of West German plasma banks paying trifling sums to East Germans in need of hard currency—the alternative newspaper *taz* ran the headline: WESTERN VAMPIRES SUCK EAST GERMAN BLOOD.

Meanwhile, the influx of West German investors is creating a room shortage in the hard-currency luxury hotels of the East. They swap stories in the hotel dining rooms. A travel agent from Saarbrücken told me over breakfast about his field work in the domain of the planned economy. It's clear that his ethnological interests have, momentarily, displaced his financial ones. He has had to set aside his intention of creating a joint venture with East German and Polish travel agencies. For now, he's just traveling around, tutoring his future partners in business management—which, he assures me, is no easy task. He has to begin literally at square one, explaining everything: chambers of commerce, trade licenses, balance sheets, ad campaigns. "Forty years of communism has done more structural damage than the war. Nothing works." He's convinced that people are deluded concerning the pace of reconstruction. "They're doing their best," he says as he wipes some caviar off his chin, "but they'll still have to pass through their vale of tears."

The man is right: there's no question that hard times lie ahead, and that the old socialist routine is in a rut. But many will be happy to know that there is at least one part of the system that is bound to survive, namely nepotism, because it is deeply rooted in the West as well. And that's not all. Wherever the socialist experiment coincided with the personal interests of a majority of test subjects, its effects will be long-lasting. The right to work, guaranteed by the East German constitution, has been sacrificed to unification. But it can't be erased so easily from the collective consciousness. Some experts predict that converting to a market economy will cost at least two million East Germans their jobs; other estimates run as high as five million. The majority of the East German electorate has announced its willingness to absorb this high cost as the price of reform. But now that it is actually happening, people are recalling the advantages they have abandoned: low rents, guaranteed employment, the slower work pace, the protective (if also tyrannical) state, which certainly deprived its wards of any voice but also relieved them of all anxiety about the future. Whatever judgment East Germans ultimately pronounce on their forty-year-long socialist experience, they did live as a society of equals—at least compared to the Federal Republic. It doesn't take a crystal ball to see how this situation might prove socially explosive. In an economic crisis, the East Germans would again find themselves second-class citizens—but with an ideology of equality. Presumably right-wing populists would be more successful in exploiting the resultant tension than left-wing agitators; in any case, a conflict would definitely ensue.

VII. Prognoses and Diagnoses

Now that the East German stage has been swept clear of Lenin and Marx, it is open for the latest gurus of the scientific age: the psychotherapists and statisticians. Although the socialist state never officially acknowledged the existence of the "unconscious," local researchers have nevertheless been preparing clandestinely for their debut. Dr. Hans Joachim Maaz, chief of psychotherapy at the Protestant Social Services Foundation in Halle (East Germany), made headlines with his findings that "the average East German citizen is dependent on authority, emotionally repressed, and, above all, incapable of experiencing pleasure."

This diagnosis bears an uncanny resemblance to popular Italian and French conceptions of Germans in general; and, like most sociopsychological findings, it also smacks of pub philosophy. First of all, as far as experiencing pleasure goes, that depends entirely on one's definition. Another East German professor, from Leipzig, has reportedly found that "the rate of orgasms in the Eastern part of Germany is substantially higher" than in the West: 37 percent of the East German women questioned achieved orgasm almost every time they had sex, while only twenty-six out of a hundred of their West German sisters could claim similar success. The East

German News Agency reported these findings under a patriotic banner headline: EXPERTS FEAR COOLING OF EAST GERMAN SEX. The Western tabloid *Bild*, on the other hand, didn't consider the news worth more than one or two small paragraphs.

Evidently all "scientific" findings on character structure must be taken with a grain of salt: Dr. Maaz's other proclaimed East German traits also require clarification. Just because people lived under dictatorships for fifty-six years doesn't necessarily mean they are "dependent on authority" and "emotionally repressed." In fact, one can draw the exact opposite conclusion: it was precisely the dictatorship that forced East Germans to put a hedge around their private lives, to develop their inner world—the one untouched by authority—to a degree far greater than did Germans living in the Western democracy. Everyone who took the opportunity to actually talk to East Germans during the first days and months of the upheavals was amazed at the emotional directness of their comments. Their stories had an existential urgency, a poignancy which left Westerners without reply. What is there to say when a gray-haired engineer describes the ruin of his professional life, how his greatest achievement lay in reinventing basic microelectronics technology using inadequate tools—all because of the Western embargo? What is there to say when grown-up men and women—unpracticed in this kind of talk—declare their whole lives wasted: "We can't manage by ourselves, we need help!" These people weren't just after something. Their words were just an honest attempt to express decades of unarticulated experience.

The Deep-Freeze Theory and Other Hypotheses

There seems to me a good deal of sense in the observations of Heike Berger, an East German specialist in psychiatry and neurology. She sees the "general loss of all values" which East Germans are now experiencing as an opportunity. "In times like these, it is hardly pathological for people to feel unsure and anxious. It would be abnormal if they didn't. As far as I'm concerned, uncertainty is the most appropriate emotion at the moment." Whether the elusive potential of this psychological openness will be realized or not will primarily depend on West German sensitivity and understanding. Let us hope the chance for change survives the changes.

Far less threatened by extinction is the East German woman. In fact, she is the one cultural product the country can be proud of. To the West German male, scarred by the battle of the sexes, she is a riddle: professionally active, self-assured, a decision-maker yet still feminine— he doesn't understand the mix. And what's more, she still desires men, though not necessarily him, the West German "softie" who so admires her.

Following the teachings of the master, Friedrich Engels, that emancipation begins in the sphere of production, the socialist state took a serious approach to women's liberation. More than 90 percent of East German women are employed; in West Germany, the figure is below 50 percent. Moreover, East Germany spared little expense to ensure equal opportunity for its women. A wealth of social programs helped ease the tensions between career demands and motherhood: daycare was provided at practically no cost, maternity leave lasted for one year at full pay, job security was guaranteed, and women enjoyed complete freedom of choice concerning pregnancy and abortion. Should any attempt be made in a unified Germany to curtail this last right, a war every bit as fierce as in the United States would ensue. East German women are not prepared to let the unifiers buy out their right to determine what happens to their bodies. In this matter they are supported by their sisters in the West, who are presently engaged in a struggle to legalize abortion in the first trimester.

In other matters, however, East and West German women disagree, and these disagreements stem from a general cultural gap. West German women criticize their Eastern sisters for continuing to relieve their men of child-raising and household chores. The Easterners counter that while women in the West have succeeded in getting their husbands to cook and change diapers, they continue to depend on them economically. But there's one area in particular where they not only don't see eye to eye, but barely speak the same language—their taste in men. The East German woman will admit that when it comes to housework and child-rearing she's still living in the nineteenth century, but she doesn't see the answer to her problem in Western-style domestic equality. The new sensitive man who has become so common in Western Europe and the northern United States is anathema to her—she'll take the first East German roughneck over him any day.

In fact, under the wings of the strong yet domestically traditional East German woman, a prehistoric male species has survived: the East German macho. For him I see little chance of survival. This is not to say that he has completely disappeared from the Western zoo. But in the West, the true, unadulterated macho can now be spotted only in the underworld. The great male mass has surrendered to the demands of equality and is now exhibiting symptoms of withdrawal. To the astonishment of his East German counterpart, the West German male (of, say, forty and under) changes diapers adroitly, cooks tolerably, and even does the dishes on occasion; he discusses with his wife or girlfriend who can go out on a given evening and who has to stay home with the kids; he participates in contraception. He's the ideal man— but not to the East German woman. Sure she compliments him, but basically she thinks he's a wimp. His biggest shock, however, comes when he meets her boyfriend, the East German macho. What is such a beautiful, desirable, emancipated woman doing with a dinosaur like this? In fact, our enlightened Western man feels more threatened by Eastern he-men than by Western feminists. Just as freshly weaned smokers are especially allergic to cigarette smoke, it pains our West German hero to see his Eastern brother blithely exploiting as weapons of sexual competition the same male vices he has worked so hard to overcome. It's a mystery, all right, for what does this Neanderthal have to offer? He puts his feet on the table, demands to be waited on, earns less than his wife, doesn't even think of cooking, washing dishes, or changing diapers—and still he is preferred, even loved? He must have something going for him that the West

German man cannot comprehend and the East German woman will not reveal.

It's inevitable that two diverse historical experiences will express themselves in the psyche and conduct of the people, both as real and projected differences. It's also clear that in the current confrontation of East and West, the East Germans will have to do the bulk of the adapting. In their drive to adapt, however, they must recognize which traits are worth preserving and be prepared to defend them, to confront whatever criticism may emerge from the other side, instead of simply letting all differences melt away in one great unity caldron. For the differences themselves could prove exciting, and promise curious collisions, amusing entanglements, and productive debates.

The last sections of Wall have now been torn down. Dozens of streets are being rejoined, abandoned subway stations revived. The city where everything was doubled—town halls, TV towers, zoos, inhabitants—is acquiring a unified and uniform face. Even before the all-Berlin election of December 1990, the two mayors united in an agreement to have the Wall completely dismantled—except for one section in the North, a decision that provoked protests from both sides of the neighborhood. One wonders why they didn't select the historic center of the city, near the Reichstag, for instance. Why not leave a piece of the Wall there, a little piece of history?

The Berlin Wall was the last tangible reminder of the war caused by the Germans, a sign of their common guilt.

Removing it completely may also remove the memory of that guilt and pave the way for the successful marketing of East Germany's most deplorable product: the German with a Clear Conscience.

We have finally been released. A normal nation again at last. Who can find fault with us now? Of course we understand our neighbors' anxieties, but they are hopelessly out of date. These historical anxieties are just a disguise for their fear of our diligence—and their own sloppiness. There's no law against becoming an economic superpower; after all, the market decides. By the way—and this is addressed to you, Allied victors—no one is forced to play number one who can't afford it. Sure, it's a little strange that the war's two major losers, Japan and Germany, are emerging forty-five years later as the actual winners. You can find some of the reasons in Marx and Engels, and besides, everybody knows that history isn't just. So are we interested in a new armed conquest of Europe? You don't even believe that yourself. As it turns out, we no longer need to resort to force.

This is the nightmare version of German unification. But there's also an optimistic version. It could turn out that normalization might actually make the Germans themselves more normal, more self-assured—in the generous sense of the word: more tolerant, more hospitable, more cheerful. In short—one hardly dares write it—happier. The uncanny efficiency of the Germans after the war grew from the same roots as the fascist cult of obedience: general unhappiness, resentment, and all the attendant virtues and vices—discipline, punctuality, self-righteousness, and that "I know better" attitude. Unhappy nations are always dangerous, even when they're rich. But for the first time in recent history the Germans have no "knife in the back," no Versailles, not even a Wall—nothing that might trigger their fear of encirclement. If anything, the enormous uncertainties of unification are bound to disarm the fundamental German craving for security. German order is now faced with a more Italian entropy: chaos, disorder, crime—all Made in Germany. Perhaps, as a result, life will be a little more relaxed, people a little more joyful.

It's not easy to believe in this optimistic scenario. But, as things stand, there is little choice but to hope for it.

Three Bad Reasons
and Two Good Ones
to Fear the Germans

When asked what he felt about German unification, the Polish writer Jacek Bocheński answered with a paradox. He couldn't hide the fact that the mere thought sent shivers down his spine—and this was precisely why he was so much in favor. For even more disturbing was the thought of what the Germans might do if their neighbors now tried to stop them from unifying.

I presume that a similar sentiment was hiding between the lines of many a congratulatory telegram from abroad, and that while many prominent people were shaking hands with Chancellor Kohl, their arms were breaking out in goose bumps.

Whoever maintains that Bocheński's worries are out of date, that the Germans have outgrown their old encirclement complex, has not read the tabloid *Bild*, the largest (West) German news daily, with a circulation of four million. Since the day the Wall opened, a black-red-gold border has graced every edition, and the articles offer display after display of traditional German *ressentiment*, cleaned of any recent lint and polished to a shine. NOW WE KNOW WHO OUR FRIENDS REALLY ARE, ran a December 15, 1989, headline, while the accompanying text graded the trustworthiness of certain neighboring nations solely on their position toward German unity. England's Maggie Thatcher failed miserably ("Does she really believe that Rhodesia has earned the right to self-determination and Germany hasn't?"), as did Italy's Giulio Andreotti ("what insolence" . . . "full of arrogance"). And while the French and the Dutch did a little better, the only candidates to receive an "A" were President Bush ("for insuring that the idea of unification stayed high on the agenda") and President Gorbachev ("A long-term friend. Hopefully he won't run out of breath").

Editorials in the more respectable *Spiegel* exhibited a similar paranoia weeks before the *Bild*. "The old attitude just won't go away: every nation but Germany is allowed to pursue its interests. And yet we are not nearly as nationalistic as the four Allied victors, or Japan, or even Italy—and we won't be, even as an economic Euro-power. All traces of our chauvinism have been effectively eradicated. We no longer want conquests, neither by war nor by peaceful means. We don't want any A-bombs or B-bombs or C-bombs. But, by the same token, we don't want to be treated like underdogs anymore, forty-five years after the war."

Der Underdog—that's the new German word for an old German feeling of having received the short end of the stick, the sentiment at the root of every outbreak of German nationalism: We're surrounded by enemies, encircled, we're always denied what everyone else is granted!

It's not surprising that the opening of the Wall sparked feelings very different from those on the day of German reunification. November 9 marked the liberation from the past, from the Wall, from the Communist dictatorship, from the division of Europe, from a hated identity that had been imposed by force. October 3, on the other hand, focused on the future; it promised freedom to construct a new national and cultural identity. It is completely understandable that the first date unleashed general jubilation, while the second set off unease and uncertainty—and not only among the victims of recent German history. Germans themselves, from both sides of the now invisible Wall, were gripped by the sense that something new and unpredictable was under way; West Germans in particular began to worry that their sense of security, their acquired amenities, were being twisted out of their hands by their brothers and sisters from the East. And they had good cause to worry, for reunification not only means the end of the East German state: it also spells the finish of the old Federal Republic.

This much has to be granted: the leading European politicians put on a rather embarrassing performance in the days and weeks preceding October 3, as it became increasingly clear that unification was inevitable. It's not that they should be taken to task for paying forty years of lip service to German unity and then suddenly beating a retreat when the moment approached. Such defensive reflexes can only be counted as natural, considering the history of Germany over the last century. What was embarrassing was that they were obviously afraid to express their completely justified concerns openly, and instead preferred to act behind the scenes in an elaborate dance of hesitation and delay.

François Mitterrand, for instance, seemed right out of Molière. One moment he was attesting to the German right to self-determination and unification, and in the next moment he was off to East Berlin to support Hans Modrow, the head of the interim government, an outspoken advocate of two German states. Andreotti's *faux pas* were equally unfortunate. A few years ago he had rubbed Germans the wrong way with the bold assertion that "the present division of one nation into two states is a fact." Once unification couldn't be stopped, he sent his prompt congratulations while simultaneously working to forestall the inevitable as long as possible with silent but tireless maneuvering at NATO and Common Market summits. Even the heroic Maggie Thatcher blanched at the prospect of a unified Germany. First she displayed her famous lack of tact by officially declaring that a unified Germany was something that could at best be discussed "in fifteen years." But when her minister of finance, Nicholas Ridley—his tongue loosened, admittedly, by several glasses of wine—translated the fears of his boss into plain pub English, he was dismissed. According to him, unification was "a German racket designed to take over the whole of Europe." He warned of the German tendency to be "uppity" and then explained with refreshing but, as it turned out, suicidal precision, that he wasn't really "against giving up sovereignty in principle—but not to this lot. You might as well give it to Adolf Hitler, frankly."

Helmut Kohl, the direct target of Ridley's remarks, reacted with amazing tranquility, recalling perhaps the long list of his own slips (which include a comparison between Gorbachev and Goebbels). I, on the other hand, was alarmed—not so much by Ridley's statements as by his dismissal.

Can people no longer exaggerate? When an English minister can no longer say aloud what many Europeans think about the Germans, we are clearly heading for deadly serious times. In retrospect, Ridley's dismissal seemed only to prove his point about German predominance. And the first shadow that the dominant continental power cast over the island kingdom was the shadow of humorlessness. Amid all the excited fluttering of suspicions and excuses, one very obvious truth went completely forgotten: if a nation has aroused certain "fears" among its neighbors through wars of aggression and genocide, then it is up to that same nation to establish its harmless intentions. Moreover, this rule must hold true for all such fears, both "rational, acceptable" ones (e.g., Germany will become an economic superpower and might misuse its strength) as well as the "malicious" and "insulting" fears such as Ridley's. Besides, as every armchair psychiatrist knows, traumatically induced fears can be dismantled only if they are expressed and worked through. And a general willingness on the part of the Germans to acknowledge their neighbors' fears would be a significant sign that such fears really are unfounded.

The agitation and verbal confusion of the European

leaders also had its tragicomic aspect: the representatives didn't realize that their constituents had long ago made up their minds. The surprising result of all the polls is that the European peoples—by contrast with their political and intellectual elites—were decidedly in favor of German unity. According to a poll published in January 1990 in *Le Soir*, 78 percent of Europeans responded to German unification positively—and this before it became an actuality. In fact, the citizens of many Common Market countries (Italy, Spain, England, Portugal, and Greece) were more enthusiastic than the West Germans.

The strongest public debates in Western Europe occurred in France and Great Britain. But here too, the warnings and objections were confined to the intellectual elite. To the surprise of most observers, 70 percent of the French and 60 percent of the British were for unification. If one is to believe the statisticians, only three groups expressed overwhelming doubt and concern: the Poles, the Russians, and the Jews, the three peoples who suffered most at the hands of the Germans.

Where do all these statistical speculations lead? First, to this: only idiots, who do of course populate the planet in sizable numbers, would draw any ironclad conclusions from such polls. For instance, the desperate "yes" of my friend Bocheński on the question of German unification would be registered by the pollsters with statistic brutality as agreement, while all his hidden objections and qualifications would be discounted as "not computable." As the American political scientist Andrei S. Markovits says: "Invisible dimensions are clearly at work in the fears about German unification. Thus we will never be able to grasp them fully; the best we can do is intuit them emotionally."

It's also true that statistics concerning the hopes and fears of the majority say nothing about whether these sentiments are justified. The fact that a majority prefers to hope does not disprove all danger; similarly, the discovery that an informed minority dreads the worst says nothing about the accuracy of this fear

Nonetheless, it is noteworthy that the historically founded fears of German unification—so vivid for the intellectual elite—don't seem to play any role in shaping the opinion of the large majority. What does this mean? Does the average citizen forgive more quickly than the intellectual? Or is the popular memory simply not as keen? Does the surprisingly positive European reaction stem from the fact that the large majority of people questioned had no direct experience of Nazi terror? Or do ordinary mortals simply doubt that history repeats itself, and therefore see no reason to learn from it?

As far as this last question is concerned, I, for my part, am convinced that history does give repeat performances—but only after a change of costume. It always reappears wearing radically different pants, jackets, and hats; most of all, history likes to take the stage as its exact opposite. That's why it makes a fool of anyone who chooses to sit and wait for the same old spectres to enter by the doors they exited forty-five years ago.

With this caveat in mind, let's look more closely at some of the fears German unification has elicited.

1. One common fear concerns the sheer size of the new Germany—the agglomeration of people, land, resources, and economic output. The fact that the Federal Republic will be dramatically enlarged, both in area and population, is interpreted to mean that Germany will soon become a superpower. Some go so far as to maintain that the united Germany will take the place of the declining U.S.A. as the world's predominant power, and warnings about a "Fourth Reich" are not infrequent.

Although I have a weakness for fears of all kinds, this particular one doesn't move me very much. I can only surmise that it stems from a lack of information. Many commentators have overlooked the simple fact that there has never been a united Germany in this form; the world is faced not so much with a "reunification" as with a "new unification." It's true that the Federal Republic has grown in size by 50 percent, but it is still *smaller* than all previous German Reichs. As of October 3, 1990, the German state covers 360,000 square kilometers (approx. 140,000 square miles)—less land than France, Spain, or Sweden. It's also true that even before unification, the Federal Republic was the strongest European economic power. But its gross national product of approximately $1.8 trillion doesn't come to even half of the American GNP.

This lack of information extends also to the economic health of the old Democratic Republic, which has been grotesquely overestimated. It is a curious anomaly of modern history that both the giant Soviet Union and tiny East Germany managed for decades to deceive Western experts and all their satellites, computers, and intelligence networks. Even professional anti-Communists grossly exaggerated the socialist economic output. In a *New Yorker* article entitled "Reflections after Communism," economist Robert Heilbroner reported a comical quarrel: "At a recent meeting near Washington, Soviet economists from the prestigious Academy of Science disputed the 'pessimistic' conclusions of the CIA that the Soviet GNP was today only between one-half and one-third as high as that of the United States. . . . The Soviet experts maintained that a truer measure put the Soviet GNP at one-seventh of the American—a figure that yields a per capita standard of living in the Soviet Union which is approximately that of China."

The CIA's incredible overestimation of Soviet economic muscle may be traced to the strong interests and influence of the Pentagon; other reasons must be sought to explain why civilian experts were equally mistaken. Evidently there is nothing more difficult for academics than to admit that they do not and cannot know anything for certain about their specialty, despite all their labors. Yet it is precisely this awareness that should have guided the gathering of economic data on the Eastern bloc. Official East German statistics were generally acknowledged to be inflated. But evidently even false statistics are better than no statistics, and so, after a few detours, the beautified numbers finally made their way into Western scholarly treatises on the East German economy.

The first people to realize the full extent of this falsification were investors from West Germany conducting field research in their new potential market. It turns out that East German productivity was at most a third and probably a fourth that of West Germany. The state of industrial technology, the infrastructure, the city buildings—all resemble their West German counterparts of forty years ago. The current economic output of all five newly federated Eastern states *combined* is equal to that of the Saarland, a tiny Western province on the French border. Many in the West have long regarded East Germany as the world's tenth strongest economic power; by that logic, the tiny state of Saarland would also rank in the top ten.

The per capita income of the Federal Republic is bound to sink after merger with such a lackluster partner. If all goes well, the East German lands may, in ten or fifteen years, attain economic parity with the largest Western province, Nordrhein-Westfalen. But even that wouldn't enable the country to keep up with Japan or the U.S.A.

Still, it cannot be denied that the new republic will be without competition in Europe, and in this sense, unification signals a setback for the continent. The uniqueness of Europe is that it contains a plethora of independent cultures, languages, and ways of life within the smallest space. And it just sounds bad when, in a chorus of five nearly equal voices, one voice suddenly drowns out the others. This has nothing to do with the nationality of the voice, and would hold just as true if France, England, Italy, or Spain suddenly burgeoned in size.

2. The tradition of German militarism provides another cause for alarm. While such a fear is historically programmed and perfectly understandable, it can also blind

against more real dangers—as we shall later see. In fact, the Germans are far from having military dreams, as was proven during the war in the Persian Gulf, specifically by the curious events surrounding the token deployment of a German squadron to Turkey.

The world was amazed to realize that the very nation that still caused its neighbors to shake with fear on the day of unification currently possesses what may be the least motivated army around. When Squadron 43 flew its Alpha jets into the Turkish strong point of Erhac, the German leadership immediately objected to being stationed directly on the border, and protested the unreasonable command. The troops' morale seemed completely disproportionate to their equipment, though, to tell the truth, the Germans were pretty far behind with that as well. A Turkish commander wondered publicly how he could protect the Germans if things got serious, since their planes were really only so much scrap metal.

Back home, professional soldiers suddenly realized that their occupation carried with it the risk of premature death, and hundreds refused to fight. Tens of thousands of drafted men followed suit. The troops stationed in Turkey told TV audiences that four weeks' work had worn them out, that they had had enough and wanted to go home. Of course, the officers in the field reassured the press that none of the army psychologists needed to be "activated"—although even they could not deny observing more and more "anxious faces." Experts criticized the Defense Ministry: none of the military's required courses had addressed the possibility that German soldiers might actually have to kill and be killed in battle.

The discovery that the most feared army of recent history had inherited more from Schweyk than Blücher was noted by Germany's neighbors—above all by the English—first with amazement and then with growing scorn. Inasmuch as this scorn was directed against a moral double standard—first the Germans sell rockets and chemical and biological weapons, and then they play the delicate peace-dove who can't bear the sight of blood—it is more than justified. But there's something else going on, something I would call "disappointed fear": How can the same Germans who so recently made the whole world tremble now be shitting in their pants?

With all due respect for our neighbors: What can they possibly expect? After a war which the Germans started and then lost, and which cost fifty million lives, the Germans have learned better than anybody else that war is something to be avoided under any circumstance. The children and grandchildren of the Nazi generation grew up with this antiwar reflex, and I consider that historical progress. Compared to the bloody fanatics of fifty years ago, the sensitive, tormented German draftee should be a welcome change to the rest of the world.

3. Will German nationalism revive following unification? I would like to clarify the question at the root of this fear before I try to answer it. How can we be so sure that for the past four decades the Germans really have been free from nationalist sentiment? This assumption is mostly based on moralistic wish fulfillment: the nation responsible for the Second World War and the Holocaust must perforce suffer enormous guilt and a permanent

inability to develop a positive self-image. If, indeed, this ever was the case, the logic definitely seems passé now. In a poll recently published by *Der Spiegel*, 66 percent of the East Germans and 68 percent of the West Germans confessed they were "proud of being a German." Only 16 percent on either side of the Wall were "not very proud." It's true I don't have comparable data for the Italians or the French; I also doubt whether anyone ever felt the need to measure the "national feeling" of these peoples. My guess is that theirs is only slightly higher—if at all.

There's really only one statistic in the German study worth noting, the one which points to the difference between West and East Germans: 5 percent of East Germans but 9 percent of West Germans stated they were "not at all proud." Evidently almost twice as many West Germans have problems with their fatherland as East Germans. It is significant, however, that only a tiny minority has any difficulty whatsoever. There is no basis for the assumption that German national pride mushroomed overnight. It is a myth that the Germans have developed an incurable insecurity complex as a result of the Holocaust. As we have seen, this diagnosis applies only to a tiny, if eloquent, minority which has in good faith projected its own troubles with the German past onto the German people. The silent majority, so it seems, has long subscribed to the sentiment expressed by Franz Joseph Strauss: "A nation that has achieved as much as we Germans have achieved has a right not to be constantly reminded about Auschwitz."

The question must also be inverted: What does it

mean, and how is it possible, that Germans today can say—despite Auschwitz—that they are proud of being German? Many sociologists have already provided the answer: denial and suppression. It is simply impossible, they say, to have both an awareness of the Holocaust and a "healthy national consciousness" at the same time.

This realization leads to a paradoxical answer to the question posed above about a revival of German nationalism. For it is precisely because the Germans haven't been suffering from any complexes—as far as their nationalist feeling is concerned—that they had no "catching up" to do at the time of unification. Moreover, on October 3, 1990, the Germans found themselves in an entirely new situation. Their traditional aggressive nationalism had mostly been a form of compensation: it drew its nourishment from the *absence* of a German national state. The three German Reichs came into being only through wars of aggression and together attained a lifespan of no more than eighty-four years. In 1990, for the first time in modern history, the Germans celebrated their "unity" peacefully and in complete accord with their neighbors. The happy festival of unification held last fall could mark the beginning of a new era: October 3 could become the birthday for a boringly normal form of nationalism that no longer draws its energy from the desire for revenge or the feeling of having come up short. The new, united Germans cannot complain to anybody. They were lucky and they know it.

Upon closer inspection, then, these traditional, historically justified fears of the Germans prove unfounded.

Three Bad Reasons and Two Good Ones

Actually everybody already knew that anyway. It was never very likely that Nazism would become attractive following its catastrophic defeat—children who have once been burned really are twice shy, especially well-behaved German children. It was equally unlikely that the old German militarism and nationalism would ever again rise triumphant—now that the whole world has been trained in early detection of these ills. What was and is much more likely is that the old diseases, unless they are thoroughly treated, will reappear in new, surprising strains not covered in any textbook. And since such metamorphoses take place over long periods of time, almost imperceptibly, the patient generally never notices. The postwar era offers peculiar examples of history returning as its opposite. Certain structural elements of Nazism, for instance, were kept marvelously intact under the invisible cap of East German antifascism: the ideological drilling of young children, the cult of personality, the practice of collective punishment against people associated with those convicted of "fleeing the republic," the culture of "living images" at sport performances, the general militarization of society, and the climate of denunciation and surveillance, which ultimately led to the idea of camps for "negative-hostile elements."

Less familiar are the disguises assumed by inherited fascist tendencies in West Germany. A strange turnaround happened here as well. Instead of the feared inclination toward militarism, there was an amazing, almost uncanny love of peace; instead of aggressive nationalism, there was an enthusiasm for Europe; instead of megalomania and haughtiness, a fanatical solidarity with trees and animals.

And here we come to the two good reasons to fear the united Germans.

1. Although I discount the fear of classical anti-Semitism, new forms of it seem to be developing. Reports of anti-Jewish slogans, graffiti, and desecrations of cemeteries are on the rise in both parts of Germany. In the West, anti-Semitism became public with the appearance of the *Republikaner*, the skinheads, and a few other neo-Nazi organizations. In the East, the government generally covered up any evidence of similar incidents; as a result, the anti-Semitism now surfacing there is all the more rabid.

Wolfgang Brück of the Leipzig Central Institute for Youth Study made a cogent observation: "In all the trials I have witnessed involving anti-Semitic incidents, the juvenile offenders responded in the negative when asked whether they personally knew any Jews." In many cases, it turned out that the authors of anti-Semitic graffiti were children of high party officials or Stasi officers. Upon closer questioning, they confessed that they really weren't aiming at the Jews at all, but at their fathers.

Of course, that's no consolation and no reason for complacency. Who can be sure that the Nazi hatred of Jews did not have similar motivations? It is often the case with anti-Semitism and racism that the specific victims are not "really" intended at all, that they stand for "something else." Not that this insight ever prevented a single pogrom. Still, there are striking differences between today's Germany and the Weimar Republic. First: present-day German anti-Semites have to make do with virtually no Jews. Before they were hunted down and murdered, about 600,000 Jews lived in Germany; now there are between 30,000 and 50,000. It's true that, in principle, you don't need even a single Jew to be anti-Semitic. Nonetheless, I'm willing to bet that classical anti-Semitism has little chance of catching on. Its monstrous history in Germany discredited it so much that it became *verboten* and is now thwarted by German obedience, if nothing else.

Which is not to say it has been overcome. There's considerable evidence that, in Germany, anti-Semitism will simply change its visage and reappear in a more symbolic, narcissistic guise. Once again, this has to do with the amazingly unflappable German self-esteem mentioned above, which can only be explained by a repression of the past. What is most upsetting to this self-esteem is the history of Jews in Germany, since this is what poses the greatest obstacle to the united Germans becoming part of the family of nations. Consequently, the new, symbolic anti-Semite will not hate actual living Jews; he will hate Jews as the descendants of the murdered Jews, the eternal witnesses testifying to the unprecedented crimes of the past. This narcissistic anti-Semite says: I want to get rid of you because you tarnish my self-image.

I suspect that a good portion of the anti-Jewish graffiti and incidents in Germany are expressions of this symbolic and narcissistic anti-Semitism. Jewish graves are desecrated to prove that "the past is past," that people are "no longer letting themselves be intimidated," that they are "free from scruples and guilt." Even among intellectuals one can find signs of this narcissistic anti-Semitism that is really directed against the past. The "historians' debate" offered a foretaste with Ernst Nolte's attempt to relativize Nazi crimes. The filmmaker Hans Jürgen Syberberg has now provided another example—which surprised only his blind admirers. I do not believe Syberberg was an anti-Semite when he made his grotesquely overrated, eight-hour film on Hitler, although even then I was struck by certain remarks which made it difficult to separate his empathetic interest in Hitler and Nazism from fascination or even admiration. Ultimately Syberberg was unable to withstand the extreme proximity to his subject, and fell into its gravitational field. Now he maintains quite openly that the Jews and the leftists are to blame for the fact that reunification took as long as it did. I'm not at all sure that Syberberg really believes his own opinion. He seems to propose anti-Semitism as a postmodern gesture of defiance, along the lines of: Maybe I don't have anything against the Jews, but I can afford to talk the way I do. The rest of you, the whole lot of you, are all just afraid and intimidated.

A Jewish rabbi best explained the mainspring of this narcissistic anti-Semitism: the Germans will never forgive us for their having gassed us at Auschwitz.

German xenophobia has a simpler structure and consequently appears without any cosmetic disguise. Many Germans utter their prejudices blatantly and unambiguously as soon as they run into foreign workers or visitors or people from Central and Eastern Europe who have sought asylum in Germany. In an East Berlin subway station, skinheads beat four Vietnamese half-dead with wooden sticks; one of the perpetrators filmed the scene on videotape. In the five Eastern provinces, right-wing radicals systematically attack homes for refugees and foreigners, smearing the walls with nationalist and racist slogans: "Germany for Germans," and even "You will soon burn!" The author of the latter was recently asked on a TV talk show whether he really meant it. He looked straight into the camera and said: "Yes."

It's not these actions, but the prejudices they express that are condoned by a great majority of East German youth. According to a study published in *Der Spiegel*, more than 40 percent of East German schoolchildren are of the opinion that there are too many foreigners in East Germany, and what's more, they feel disturbed by this foreign presence. This statistic seems all the more alarming when we recall that only 160,000 foreigners actually reside in the former Democratic Republic, less than 1 percent of the population.

But although the xenophobia in united Germany strongly recalls well-known German inclinations—for example, the megalomania of the Nazis—I hesitate to say it actually derives from these earlier tendencies. The growing intolerance toward foreigners is a European phenomenon, and in certain respects is a direct result of November 9, 1989. For now that the Wall is open, the poor of Europe are suing for the promise of a better life. As they cross the various borders into the West they realize that they now face a new wall: the wall between the rich and the poor. The question of how the rich countries of Europe will deal with the onslaught from the poor countries is Political Problem Number One for the coming decade. But this is not specifically a German problem.

2. A further fear concerns the stability of democracy in Germany—the question posed by the Turkish writer Aras Ören. After the Wall opened, the East Germans managed to discard in literally a few weeks the norms and patterns of behavior they had acquired over decades. This impressive shedding naturally invites the counterquestion: Could a serious crisis cause the West Germans to "forget" their democracy just as quickly and reach back to old, authoritarian patterns?

The likelihood of this occurring is not very great, for, by contrast with East Germany, West Germany provided its citizens and the world with the model of a functioning democracy of undisputed economic success. This is the reason why the Federal Republic would undoubtedly be defended in case of danger.

Such optimism should be tempered, however, with a healthy dose of reservation. As is well known, democracy was imported into West Germany from America, France, and England following the unconditional capitulation of the Nazis. In East Germany it succeeded the total economic and political collapse of socialism. Of course, its beginnings can be traced to a genuine popular uprising, but the dominant model is once again an import, this time from West Germany.

Naturally, an imported democracy is unquestionably preferable to any type of dictatorship, whether home-grown or imported. The problem in the German case is that democracy was accepted because and to the extent that it was economically successful. While the value of democracy is tied to its economic success all over the world, in Germany this is particularly true. In East Germany, too, democracy will find acceptance only if and to the extent that it produces results. No one yet knows how tenaciously Germans East or West will defend their democracy in the event of an economic crunch. In other words, no one knows how far they will go to protect the nonmaterial merits of democracy if the cash box runs low. Until now there has been little occasion to judge, since history has spared the Germans such a test. However, since reunification is proving much more costly than Helmut Kohl was willing to admit during elections, a test could be imminent. And the prognosis seems mixed at best.

When the Federal Republic was enlarged, its greatest defect, which may safely be called a moral vacuum, was also expanded proportionally. It used not to stand out so much; in the economically impressive, politically sub-dued West German half-state, almost everybody was happy with Helmut Kohl's schoolboy maxim: "German soil shall henceforward bring forth only peace."

Until quite recently, the West Germans got by wonderfully with their chosen leaders, who weren't so much expected to stand their ground as sit at their desks, whose venue seemed more properly the paneled study than the soapbox, who exhibited more business acumen than personal opinion. But suddenly the war in the Persian Gulf revealed the newly unified country in all its nakedness, a spectacle of embarrassments, excuses, dilettantism, simplistic statements, and readily transparent and easily contradicted expressions of innocence. The overwhelming impression was that the Germans, who historically had been associated with an overly rigid and often ruinous adherence to principles, had in the meantime developed an especially unscrupulous merchant mentality. They evidently had no qualms about delivering the deadliest of weapons to regions in crisis, while the Minister of Finance kept his eyes steadfastly shut. But when the United Nations needed them, the Germans were suddenly screening their calls, preferring instead to play angels of peace. To this end, they cited their constitution, which prohibits them from sending troops into the same "regions in crisis"—apparently even under the auspices of the UN.

However one judges the Allied intervention in the Gulf, the German equivocation is by no means new. Earlier occasions amply demonstrated how the West German government excelled in muffled responses or complete silence whenever democratic principles required defense anywhere outside German soil. Regardless of where human rights were being violated— whether in Chile, South Africa, Czechoslovakia, or Poland—the Germans in office always preferred to look the other way and say as little as possible, even when it concerned their "brothers and sisters" across the Wall. They minded their business and shut their mouths. Unobtrusiveness was the political ideal for postwar Germans; and it should also be noted that the world didn't demand or expect anything else. Whoever sought refuge from the death squads in Chile or Argentina preferred to turn to the American or French embassies rather than to the German, and that was probably well advised. I also haven't heard of one single Chinese dissident straying into the West German Embassy after the massacre at Tiananmen Square to find asylum.

Most significantly, during the ten years of struggle in Eastern Europe that preceded the events of 1989, the West German response was so phlegmatic as to make it indistinguishable from utter indifference. When the Polish trade union Solidarity was first silenced by General Jaruzelski's December coup d'état, the Social Democrats then in power, as well as a large number of intellectuals, called on the Poles to maintain calm for the sake of world peace. The total lack of German indignation at the Jaruzelski coup so outraged the French philosopher André Gorz that he hurled this sentence across the Rhine: "Freedom has no home in Germany." The only answer he received was a general sneer at "French bombast."

The same scenario repeated itself at every further opportunity. Whenever and wherever open resistance broke out beyond the Wall, the West Germans in office and the majority of their intellectuals played down the repression and advised humility for the sake of "world peace." Western support of the popular movement for peace and human rights in East Germany remained weak—this applied not only to the major parties but to a large portion of the West German peace movement and many leftist groups as well. With typically absolute German conviction they shouted for reform, détente, and peace. If the West Germans had had their way, the dictatorship in the East would likely never have been overthrown. In 1986, Władysław Bartoszewski, the recipient of the Peace Prize of the German Book Industry, voiced his concern in a speech given at the Paulskirche in Frankfurt: "It seems that in many cases, world peace is less important than individual peace and quiet, and that the concept of peace itself has become an object of manipulation."

I'm not saying that the lack of democratic reflex so evident in the highly polemical German press also characterizes the silent majority. But this majority did not express its own opinion, except perhaps in vague, mute gestures: whenever "ordinary German citizens" were challenged to show their solidarity, they loaded trucks and sent packages—hundreds of thousands of packages. That's what they did in 1982 after Jaruzelski's coup, and again in the fall of 1990 when Gorbachev requested help. Nowhere in the world is so much money collected for good causes, nowhere are so many packages packed as in Germany. It's very true, direct material help is often worth more than an incendiary appeal to democratic principles; but when packing packages is not a complement to but a routine substitute for moral and political support, then something is definitely missing.

It's an apparent paradox: the extreme pragmatism of West Germany after the war, the general mistrust of ideals, and the almost exclusive focus on economic success are the result of idealism, an exaggerated idealism, an idealism gone awry and wrecked. The same flight into a fanatic materialism—or anti-idealism—will certainly repeat itself in the Eastern part of Germany, and even a cursory examination of the former socialist state will reveal the corresponding mechanism.

Structurally speaking, East German Stalinism was identical to Stalinism in all the other countries in the Eastern bloc. What distinguished the East German variety, however, was the degree of personal dedication and faith it could elicit. Whoever reads the testimonies and confessions of former party officials and Stasi functionaries cannot escape the disquieting realization that a surprising number of party members were acting out of idealism, and participating in the work of oppression with little or no selfish interest. It turns out that faithful party comrades made up a good portion of the spying apparatus that spread through the society like some malignant disease. The public lament of many East German intellectuals over the loss of their world picture is also unparalleled in the rest of Central and Eastern Europe. In Poland, in Hungary, in Czechoslovakia, any intellectual who expressed hope in socialism after the invasion of Prague was considered either a careerist or a pathetic madman. In East Germany, on the other hand, there are a striking number of unshakable condoners, whose faith in socialism revived after every one of its many terrible defeats, and did not break down until well after the actual demise of the East German state.

The particularly East German excess of idealism and the ensuing disappointment gives rise to a "heroic" cynicism now that East Germany has entered the capitalist competition: no more ideals, no more politics, no more trust in anyone, whoever believes in anything is an idiot!

The testimony of a former Stasi collaborator exposed by two women she had informed on provides impressive proof for this model of reaction: "The things in life that were always so important to me—honesty, truth, uprightness—I saw only through the eyes of the Party, the ideal. . . . And today I ask: Who has the right to use naïve, well-intentioned people, like I always was, in such a way? I feel so angry now. And I know that I could go to the PDS* and they would give me credit for my twenty years of service. But I wouldn't even dream of doing it. Never again will I join any club or political group. I only want to speak for myself and not act in the name of any idea ever again. Of course I came to the Stasi voluntarily, I thought it was the greatest task for a party member. That's the way I was. Just a year ago I told my story to a comrade I used to know. She said that although she, too, was also a loyal comrade, she could never have done what I did. And I said to her: 'Well, so I'm a better comrade than you!' "

What is particularly German, and particularly significant, about this is the merciless logic. The woman seemed honestly convinced that she was a "better comrade" ("better" in the moral sense of the word) because she committed herself to carrying out an obviously base

---

* Party of Democratic Socialism, a spin-off of the old ruling party, read by many as "Praktisch Das Selbe" (Practically the Same Thing).

act—namely, spying on two women whom she professed to admire. By violating her ideals, she demonstrated her idealism.

It's obvious that her conclusion never to "act in the name of any idea ever again" is just as extreme as the idealism that led her to the Stasi in the first place. None of the self-imposed penitence ("never again will I join any club," etc.) will last; it will ultimately lead to new radical creeds and cures, such as the absolute faith in a profit principle that "heroically" disdains all morality.

With all due respect for the difference between the two dictatorships, the speech of the rueful Stasi agent could have come word for word out of the mouth of the average Nazi after the war. The conclusion as well: no more ideals.

In both 1945 and 1989 we see the extreme consequent of an extreme antecedent. From the past willingness to commit crimes in the name of ideals, the conclusion was, and is, drawn that ideals actually *lead* to committing crimes and must therefore be avoided. This much is certain: the West German Nazi generation derived precisely this lesson from its defeat and in the first twenty years after the war confined itself to the production of tangible goods, which were very salable: houses, cars, weapons. This focus on the strictly material was distorted only by a certain fanaticism. German weapons dealers, for example, differed little from their European and American counterparts except in their especially unscrupulous behavior. To provide a dictator who has consistently defined his goal as the annihilation of Israel with

German poison gas and missile technology forty years after the Holocaust—that took a very "heroic" disdain indeed.

The denazified founders of the Federal Republic created a moral vacuum at the center of their new capitalist economy. It was this vacuum which was challenged by the next generation, when the protest movement of 1968 reacted with an overproduction of ideology. Now, in 1991, the disappointed East Germans are jumping to the same conclusion—"no more ideals"—and there will in all probability emerge a second, highly ideological countermovement to exact its revenge.

It doesn't take much imagination to see that complications arise when two vacuums collide. Two disappointed idealists meet after forty years, each playing the trickster, the rogue—that's the stuff of comedy, as long as there's no war.

But a war there was. And the war in the Persian Gulf abruptly ruptured the political and moral communication between newly united Germany and the rest of the world. I wasn't the only one who kept waiting for my government to respond. But all in vain, for the only thing the German government managed to do was quietly pay the mandated fee (in the billions) for the criminal export of German poison. Once again, they minded their business and shut their mouths. Finally, when the end was in sight and Gorbachev presented his peace proposal, there was a reaction: in the morning, the cabinet in Bonn expressed its happy hope for the Soviet offer, and that very evening Helmut Kohl explained why the U.S.A.

had no other option but to turn the proposal down (as it had just done). This official sycophantic babble went on and on. The first foreign policy test of united Germany was a complete disaster.

The utter lack of official response was accompanied by an excess of popular conviction. The Germans were in the privileged position of being able to reflect on the events in the Gulf without any time pressure. Because the Federal Republic did not participate in the actual fighting, thanks to the constitutional clause mentioned above, there was no urgent need for hasty or unshakable positions. Nevertheless, upon my return from the U.S.A. in late January, I realized that almost everyone I knew held an exaggeratedly firm opinion that completely excluded all other points of view. No one I met confessed uncertainty; quite the contrary. My first day back I managed to destroy two long-standing friendships by not answering questions about my own position in the expected fashion. Indeed, the Gulf War swept away emotional dams in both the new and the old Federal Republics, releasing feelings whose force and one-sided focus deserve a closer look. I saw sheets spread from balconies bearing the word LIFE with no further clarification, others displayed the word FEAR, while one banner simply stated, without any direct object, STOP! Every day I read about a new initiative "for the victims of the Gulf War." In Berlin, doctors and nurses collected tons of infant formula and medications. I learned only indirectly that the term "war victim" applied solely to children in Baghdad and Amman; no one mentioned the children of Kuwait or Israel. Medical personnel in Frankfurt went so far as to declare publicly that they would refuse to treat American victims of a gas attack; they didn't want to support the Gulf War by providing such assistance.

I had the impression that the emotions the war had unleashed in the German press had little or nothing at all to do with the war itself. They were mostly expressions of self-analysis, attempts by the Germans to come to terms with themselves, and with their own experience with that other war, the one that united the entire world against the Germans.

Over and over I heard the following explanation of the German categorical condemnation of the Allied bombardment of Iraq: "We Germans know what war is." Surely no one could deny that. But didn't the others— the Dutch, the French, the English, the Czechs, all of whom participated in the war against Iraq—didn't they know just as well? Hadn't they most recently experienced war as victims of German aggression? And whence the apparently spontaneous and instinctive identification with the people of Iraq who were victims of an Allied bombing, but not the Israelis who were also bombarded? Didn't this also come from bottled-up resentment (and suffering) that had practically never been expressed throughout the forty-five years since World War II: "We too were bombarded by the Allies in a similarly senseless and barbaric fashion. And just as this war is unjust, so was the war that freed the world from Nazi fascism."

From the experience of Nazi fascism one might derive completely different lessons and priorities. For instance, that the Germans would feel a particular twinge whenever large countries occupy and swallow small ones. For instance, that the Germans would be the first to show their sympathy when a people is deprived of self-government, oppressed, and incited to several wars of aggression. Clearly such reactions did occur in the small neighboring nations that had in their time been violated by the Germans. But in the homeland of the former aggressors there was little to indicate a similar trend. What happened instead was a broad vote among Social Democrats and peace activists against war—no matter what. The Social Democrats went so far as to demand that the government withhold its approval of the UN resolution unless the use of force was excluded on principle. A few speakers from the Protestant Church went even further: "Not even Hussein's unconscionable aggression, not even his readiness to commit further genocide this time against Israel, can justify a war," stated regional superintendent Ako Haarbeck.

I have respect for consistent pacifism. What makes the above-cited German utterances unbearable is not their objection to war, but their moral double standard. The peace movement did nothing when Saddam Hussein's army marched into Kuwait, and nothing again when he threatened the Kurds with genocide following the war. Reports on Iraqi atrocities were available (from Amnesty International); every pacifist with more than half a conscience should have demonstrated in front of the Iraqi Embassy in August 1990. But apart from a handful of honest heroes, no such demonstration took place. And yet, when the Allies launched their bombs against the aggressor on January 15, 1991, hundreds of thousands gave spontaneous vent to their indignation and concern. Thus it came to a strange twist: many Germans considered the Allied attack against the Iraqi invaders as naked, unprovoked aggression, the true evil, the "greater wrong"—while the actual aggressor, Saddam Hussein, whom no one really liked, began to be seen more and more as the victim. Although the demonstrators took every occasion to assure the world they were not anti-American, their posters showed anti-American slogans impossible to overlook. AMIS OUT OF SAUDI ARABIA, AMI GO HOME. No one cared that the United States had sent troops into the Gulf in alliance with about three dozen other countries. The main thing was that the old image of the enemy, which had suffered somewhat with the collapse of socialism, once again applied: the Americans are to blame for the war.

More striking than anything that appeared on the demonstrators' posters was what did not appear: there wasn't a single word about the Scud missiles fired at Israel. Christian Ströbele, the acting speaker of the Greens, told interviewer Henryk Broder that "the Iraqi missile attacks are the logical, almost inevitable consequence of Israeli politics."

"So it's Israel's own fault if it is now being attacked with missiles?" asked Broder, unable to believe his own ears.

"It is the consequence of Israeli policy toward the Palestinians."

What most interests me in this exchange is an incidental aspect. Christian Ströbele gave this interview just before leaving for Israel on official Green business, and he gave it to Henryk Broder, the Jewish writer accredited with the discovery of "leftist anti-Semitism," which he described in a book fifteen years ago. Since that time, he has written on the subject frequently. How is it that Ströbele has such a frightfully good conscience? Where does he get his deadly honesty and candor, in short, the assumption that he might spout such true German idiocies so boldly and foolishly, and this on the eve of a trip to Israel and into the ear of a Jewish journalist known for his especially keen sense of hearing? Even a little opportunism would have been welcome, since the scruples implied in circumlocution suggest at least a bit of historical shame. Only the false good conscience of the antifascist could mislead a halfway intelligent German to express such "understanding" for missile attacks on the civilian population in Israel.

It cannot be overstated: any German peace movement, even if it is blind or one-sided, is far better than a German war movement with the same traits. But it is still by no means beyond criticism, and not always harmless. The German peace movement concealed the threat to Israel both consciously and unconsciously. Information was not lacking, the threat was not new, and it was not Saddam Hussein's invention.

German readiness for peace at any price is a reaction to (and also a form of self-punishment for) the extreme aggression of Nazi fascism. Such a swing of the pendulum is perhaps inevitable—and infinitely preferable to the historical alternative. The problem with the German pendulum is that it always tends to make extreme swings, beyond all acceptable measure. In fact, even the calculated mean would likely prove extreme. Until today this penchant for extreme swings is not yet overcome, and thus it may be some time before the Germans can register in the guest book of history as a completely normal people.

···

Of Dogs and Germans

When God created the German, He gave him the German shepherd as a companion. And I for one will not be swayed by any claim that the dog was originally Scottish or Irish, for if the German shepherd wasn't German by birth, it has certainly proven itself German by choice. At every turning point in modern German history, the shepherd has stuck to its post with steadfast determination. When Adolf Hitler was so disappointed with his Germans that he shot himself inside his bunker, he not only left his people without their *Führer*, but a German shepherd without its master—an event that inspired Günter Grass to write a 700-page novel entitled *Dog Years*. And when the Berlin Wall fell and Erich Honecker fled to the Soviet Union, he was not only abandoning seventeen million Germans, but thousands of German shepherds as well.

   Of course, it's safe to presume that Honecker had no personal relationship with his many loyal four-legged sentries; after all, they guarded not just his house in

Wandlitz, but the entire East German state. Nevertheless, these animals so closely connected with the Germans were the first to feel the wounds left by the cutting edge of history on November 9. Overnight they lost their jobs as well as their homes in the kennels along the border.

The true dimensions of their service didn't become known until after the Wall came down. All told, the East Germans kept over 5,000 dogs along the border, including approximately 2,500 watchdogs and 2,700 so-called horse dogs. They weren't all German shepherds, for in the egalitarian workers' state, these aristocrats had no choice but to share space with Rottweilers, schnauzers, and all types of mixed breeds.

Germans on both sides of the Wall were moved by the news that thousands of their favorite dogs had lost their masters during the night of November 9. They feared the worst. In the collective imagination, the desperate, forlorn dogs gathered along desolate stretches of border to howl at their one remaining employer, the moon. People even expected to see wild and dangerous packs of homeless animals prowling the suddenly accessible streets of West Berlin.

But nothing of the kind happened. Immediately after the Wall opened, the West German *Tierschutzverein* (Society for the Prevention of Cruelty to Animals) began negotiating with the East German Ministry for National Defense. After many tortuous special sessions, the Society finally announced, in January 1990, that 2,500 Wall-dogs would settle in West Germany within the following eight weeks. Hundreds of sympathetic single households along with dozens of families with children spontaneously expressed their willingness to adopt. But a shadow soon darkened this bright moment of East–West accord as the dogs became the occasion for a typically German dispute—this time between Western and Eastern shepherd experts.

The news of the impending transfer unleashed the wrath of the West German German Shepherd Association, who then accused the Society of insufficient expertise and carelessness. The Association claimed that the border dogs were much too "dangerous" for inexperienced animal lovers. They had been kept "without social contact with humans," they would become more and more "difficult to integrate into families" as they grew older, and they were "scarcely capable of being reeducated for normal daily life." Moreover, dogs that were "too heavily predispositioned" would be far better off staying "over there."

The West German mass media immediately cashed in on the excitement. Front-page articles spoke of "bloodhounds" and "killer beasts"; the dogs were described as asocial and psychologically unstable—many had even had their incisors sharpened to a fine point with a special file. One thousand were so dangerous they needed to be put to sleep. Dogs that had been raised under Stalinism were too "influenced by their environment" to be suited for house pets.

These allegations cut the East German dogkeepers to the quick, and for perhaps the first time in history, friends and foes of dogs joined hands in common protest. Experts from East German animal shelters spoke of Western smear campaigns reminiscent of the Cold War. From two pathological biters (that really did have to be put to sleep) the West German press had made 1,000— and the reasons were obvious. For if 2,500 East German dogs suddenly flooded the market—where they currently sold for about $60 apiece—the overall price would be sure to drop. In order to protect the Western purebloods from this devaluation, their Eastern brothers and sisters were being systematically defamed. Whereas in fact, the East Germans claimed, the poor border dogs were really the "last victims of Stalinism," and as such deserved special care and understanding. Far from being misanthropic, the dogs who had served with the border patrols were actually "very much in need of love" and eager for affection: since they had worked in shifts, always serving at least four different masters, they had been deprived of the special master-dog relationship. What's more, the dogs were uneducated and completely incompetent; they couldn't even bite on command. Really, they had just been "dummy dogs," running back and forth along the Wall, the harmless embodiments of their own myth— living scarecrows for humans. Not a single refugee had ever even been nipped by one of these dogs. On the contrary, every Wall-jumper who had given them a friendly click of the tongue was welcome to pet and scratch them behind the ears. These purported descendants of the Baskerville hound had only two things on their minds: a humble meal and a little tenderness. In fact, one West German buyer even returned a particularly majestic specimen, indignant that the animal hadn't uttered a peep when burglars broke into his house.

The East German defenders of the homeless border dogs grew downright alarmed when they realized that the negative propaganda had actually enticed whole flocks of undesirable buyers. Pimps looking for a "killer beast" strolled up and down in front of the East Berlin kennels; dog maniacs suffering from Napoleonic complexes saw the opportunity to compensate for their small stature by acquiring a gigantic German shepherd. Nor were prospective buyers from abroad lacking. Stories circulated about rich New Yorkers who flew Pan Am to Berlin for one day just to purchase a Wall-dog for their Fifth Avenue apartments. The head of the East Berlin Border Patrol's Canine Service told of a Spaniard who tried to acquire several dogs at once for medical experiments, of Koreans and Chinese who were eyeing the animals as major ingredients for tasty culinary specialties from down home. The orphaned dogs' East German wardens grew more suspicious with every passing day. They began to subject Western clients to oral and even written tests designed to separate "serious" dog lovers from "dubious" ones.

Unfortunately only a small number of the German shepherds could be placed in East German homes, due to the well-known shortage of living space. Moreover, forty years of antifascist training had evidently affected the taste of the East German populace, who now preferred house pets that could not possibly be identified as symbols of power, aggression, or domination: para-keets, cats, and miniature rabbits.

The dispute has now died down. Almost all the border dogs have been successfully adopted, and there's little talk of problems of integration. Many of the new arrivals who first reacted to canned food in all its Western variety with upturned noses or even diarrhea have successfully adjusted. Most have overcome their fear of elevators and escalators. They are no longer afraid of unknown canine species and have stopped running away at the sight of miniature poodles wearing knitted caps and leather jack-ets. Almost all are proving themselves willing to learn, even to the point of understanding commands in dialects other than Saxon.

But whenever they accompany their new Western masters on walks near where the Wall once stood, they are suddenly deaf to every call and run their programmed beat without veering right or left. The Wall itself has disappeared so completely that even native Berliners can't always say exactly where it used to stand. Only the Wall-dogs move as if tethered by an unseen leash, with absolute certainty, following the old border along its wild zigzags through the city—just as though they were look-ing for, or maybe missing, something . . .

But perhaps this story is only a legend—like the Wall itself.